Interactions on Digital Tablets in the Context of

3D Geometry Learning

**Human–Machine Interaction Set**

coordinated by
Jérôme Dinet

Volume 2

# Interactions on Digital Tablets in the Context of 3D Geometry Learning

David Bertolo

WILEY

First published 2016 in Great Britain and the United States by ISTE Ltd and John Wiley & Sons, Inc.

ISTE Ltd
27-37 St George's Road
London SW19 4EU
UK

www.iste.co.uk

John Wiley & Sons, Inc.
111 River Street
Hoboken, NJ 07030
USA

www.wiley.com

© ISTE Ltd 2016

Library of Congress Control Number: 2016941694

British Library Cataloguing-in-Publication Data
A CIP record for this book is available from the British Library
ISBN 978-1-84821-926-7

# Contents

# Preface

Multipoint digital terminals have grown largely in popularity over the past few years. An increasing number of schools are experimenting with the introduction of digital tablets in their classrooms in a hope that the educational experience will benefit. However, stores dedicated to these new devices have developed almost no programs for the learning of 3D geometry throughout primary and secondary schools. The main obstacle for any application of this type is the ability to manipulate three dimensions from a two-dimensional device, and hence, young students learning about spatial structures are often unable to do so with classic desktop programs. In this book, we will focus on use of the new technologies supported by digital tablets. We have several goals: allowing 9- to 15-year-old students to manipulate, observe and modify 3D spaces, as well as measuring the educational contributions of an approach that is not technology based but rather anthropo-centered.

By taking a user-centered approach, we will first suggest an interactional grammar, adapted to young learners. We will then evaluate the accessibility and the ease of both use and learning of our interactions. Finally, we will study the *in situ* educational benefits of the use of digital tablets equipped with a program based on the previously developed grammar.

We will note that by using a collection of adapted interactions, students will manipulate, observe and modify 3D spaces intuitively. Furthermore, the use of such programs during spatial geometry learning has shown to be of significant benefit to Year 5s, particularly in terms of linking perspectives and the investigation of patterns.

This book will first and foremost take a two-pronged approach, of both human–machine interactions and educational science, and then suggest a grammar and an implementable language for interactions on multi-touch digital tablets for all 3D geometry applications. All these are aimed at 9- to 15-year-old students.

I will also take an advantage of this foreword to acknowledge all the people thanks to whom the writing and the publication of this book have been made possible.

David BERTOLO
May 2016

# Introduction

## I.1. Observations and motivations

Although multipoint touchscreens have existed since the 1980s, they have only become popular over the last few years. The rapid development of smartphones and among others, in 2007 the launch of the iPhone, contributed to this rise in popularity. Following this, the recent trend for touchscreen tablets has increased, with several reports confirming the high penetration coefficient of these devices and their use in households [ARC 13, DEL 13]. These new mobile devices offer further opportunities for interaction through the integration increasing complimentary technology. Furthermore, it is now usual for smartphones and tablets, already equipped with multi-touch screens, to also be fitted with cameras and sensors of all types (accelerometer, gyroscope, compass, etc.). With the view of increasing the efficiency of their teaching, educational institutions have quickly begun integrating these technologies into their classrooms. Numerous experiments are taking place in many countries where tablets have been introduced into schools: in France, for example, in the department of Corrèze, all children entering secondary school have been equipped with an iPad. On a more general level, in 2013, Apple had already sold over 8 million iPads directly to institutions dealing with education [ETH 13]. Experience, however, shows that the advancement of learning has never been solely techno-centered. Nonetheless, the new interactive possibilities made possible by these tablets make possible new learning opportunities for certain concepts that may be able to make the most of such technologies. Among these, the one which seems to show the most promise in linking to these new interactions is without a doubt that of 3D geometry. For example, it is difficult for young students to establish the link between 3D solids and their planar representations. In parallel, many studies are focused on the manipulation of 3D spaces from 2D devices, particularly those that are also multi-touch. This observation guides us to fully investigate this lead.

## I.2. Contributions

In this context, we will show that the existing interactive 3D geometry programs are subject to limitations, particularly for 9- to 15-year-old young students. Throughout this book, our main contribution will be to show that by using a group of adapted interplays, we are able to overcome these limitations and create an ongoing link between real objects and their 3D representations for students learning about spatial structure. For this we will suggest, from a human-centered design/approach, a formal grammar as well as an interactive language adapted to the investigated theme and our target public.

Next, we will present those interplays that have been developed and show the complementarity of different installed technologies on current tablets throughout the development of an app based on our developed grammar and language.

Finally, we will show through *in situ* evaluations that when this technology is introduced into a classroom, it has educational benefits in the learning of 3D geometry.

## I.3. Book outline

This book is divided into 4 chapters and finishes with conclusions:

– Chapter 1 will describe the state of the art in learning 3D geometry. In order to conceptualize the interactions that facilitate the learning of 3D geometry, it is essential to know and understand the main elements of its teaching. This chapter will focus on the different stages of structuring the 3D space as well as the difficulties faced by the students during the learning process.

– Chapter 2 will cover the state of the art in interactions on digital terminals. After describing the use of mobile devices in our context, we will cover a brief material history before describing the group of interplays now made possible on these devices.

– Chapter 3 will first present the principle of the user-centered approach that has been the guiding thread throughout the studies described in this book. It will then describe the formal grammar that we have developed as well as the following interactive language. Finally, we will hear some user experiences to evaluate the acceptation and the ease of assimilation of our program.

– Chapter 4 will present evaluations relative to the learning of 3D geometry and show the benefits of the prototype developed based on our grammar and interactive language. As such, we will link to the first chapter by showing that in situations of discovery and investigation, we facilitate the link between real objects and their planar representations.

– Finally, the Conclusion will present our conclusions as well as the upcoming prospects for the future of our research.

1

# Construction of Spatial Representation and Perspective in Students

From a young age, children play with and manipulate solid objects such as cubes and blocks. Whether these are the first wooden blocks used by babies or later the "bricks" of all shapes used in construction games such as Lego (see Figures 1.1(a) and (b)), children observe, manipulate and use solids. They come across these objects in their day-to-day life (see Figure 1.1(c)). We could, therefore, expect that these students would be entirely familiar with the main characteristics of solids, given that they are also studied in primary and secondary education. However, in national French evaluations of Year 6 in 2011, 40% of students were unable to correctly describe a cuboid (number of faces and edges) from its representation in oblique perspective (see Figure 1.2). Similarly, nearly 50% of students were unable to complete this same task for a prism (source: French National Education).

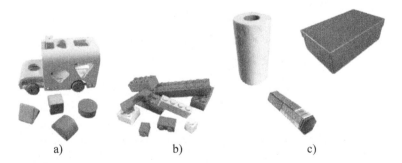

a)                    b)                    c)

**Figure 1.1.** *Solids used by children for playing or in day-to-day life: a) wooden solids; b) Lego; c) daily life*

Numerous avenues have been studied with the aim of facilitating the learning of 3D geometry – for example, the manipulation of solids in real life, as well as the use of interactive geometry programs, or more recently, the use of digital touchscreen tablets equipped with multi-touch interfaces and various sensors. An increasing number of academies in partnership with political institutions (regional, departmental, etc.) are putting experiments in place within schools, with the aim of evaluating any potential educational benefit of these new tools. These new devices have now made new interplays possible and bring new possibilities of visualization and manipulation. However, for these avenues to benefit the teaching of this complex concept, it is necessary to understand the reasons behind these difficulties in order to find ways within them to facilitate teaching. Human–computer interactions (HCI) are centered on humans, and it would be unrealistic to think it is possible to design devices to help students without understanding their obstacles beforehand and the reasons behind the obstacles.

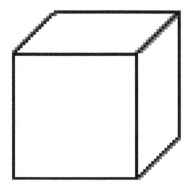

**Figure 1.2.** *For a student, what is represented? Is it a cube or a square and two parallelograms?*

In order to cover difficulties in teaching 3D geometry, we must quote Mithalal [MIT 10]:

> "3D geometry is one of the more delicate subjects within the teaching of mathematics; such is the difficulty of "seeing 3D": both for students, who can no longer use drawings to underpin their reasoning, as well as for teachers who lose the illustrative purpose of drawings. Whichever the perspective, it becomes a question of *visualization*."

In this chapter, we will "see" the causes of these problems from both a didactic and an educational viewpoint, in order to suggest relevant interactions for our audience – students aged 9 to 15 years. The didactic elements will allow us to justify the chosen age range, among other things. First, we describe spatial representation to the child according to Piaget [PIA 48]. Then, we study the representation of geometrical objects, particularly the status of drawing. From these inputs, we articulate a theory on the transition of the physical 3D object to its planar representation and conclude by describing new technologies in the learning of 3D geometry.

## 1.1. Spatial representation in children according to Piaget

### 1.1.1. *From perception to representation*

According to Piaget [PIA 47, PIA 48]:

> "The biggest difficulty in psychogenetic analysis of space concerns the fact that the progressive construction of spatial markers takes place on two distinct planes: the perceptive or sensorial-motor plane, and the representative or intellectual plane".

From birth, children construct their own sensorial-motor space that evolves alongside the development of their perception and motility. Piaget sets this period between birth and the age of two. After this, from the development of language, imagery and intuitive thinking, children progressively enter the representative space between two and seven years of age.

Piaget and Inhelder's studies have put forth three stages of development of spatial representation in children, which are based on the stages of infant drawing put forward by Luquet [LUQ 27]:

– "synthetic incapacity" between 3 and 4 years of age, at which time drawings do not correspond to perception;

– "intellectual realism" between 4 and 8 years of age, at which time children are capable of spatial analysis through observation. Spatial relationships become coordinated and projection relationships emerge;

– "visual realism" from 8-9 years onward, when children start to use perspective.

### 1.1.1.1. *Stage I: "synthetic incapacity"*

At the synthetic incapacity stage, spatial representation in children is characterized by the fact that Euclidean and projective markers are neglected. Children also do not take distances or perspectives into consideration. They begin constructing topographical reports, without necessarily mastering cases such as the drawing of a person. Among these, the following are some significant relationships:

– of "proximity" (against, close, far, etc.): this is respected in general but not in the detail of the drawings. A good example of this is the "tadpole man" studied by Luquet (see Figure 1.3);

– of "separation": children have difficulties in "separating" elements from one another, such as the edges of a quadrangle;

– of order: this only begins at this stage, allowing the better determination of the relative position in a couple. Reversals such as mouth, nose and eye types are noted (see Figure 1.3(a));

– circling or neighboring (in, inside, on, under, etc.): at this stage, children draw things such as eyes outside of the head or a roof pointing inside the house (see Figure 1.3(b));

– of continuity and discontinuity: at this stage, children are content juxtaposing elements without taking into account continuous relations, such as a hat drawn above the head of a person.

**Figure 1.3.** *a) Tadpole people, a classic example of synthetic incapacity; b) a house with an inverted roof, representing the difficulty of the neighboring relationship [LUQ 27]*

Therefore, during the stage of synthetic incapacity, topographical relationships appear without necessarily becoming generalized when it comes to complex shapes such as those children prefer to draw: people, animals, houses, etc. At this stage, the graphical space is lacking the relationships of distance and proportion; however, above those is missing directional relationships in three dimensions, and therefore, all perspective logic is missing.

### 1.1.1.2. Stage II: "intellectual realism"

Following from the synthetic incapacity, children enter a new stage named "intellectual realism". Here, children do not draw what they see of the object but rather "everything 'in it'" [LUQ 27]. Intellectual realism is a method of representation that is marked by the acquisition of topographical relationships seen during the previous stage. We may note the importance taken by neighboring relationships that are often used to mark transparence, for example, in the drawing of a duck in its egg (see Figure 1.4(a)).

Projection and Euclidean relationships are only beginning here and are used incoherently and without the coordination of points of view. When these enter into opposition with the topographical relationships, the latter will win out in the representation (see Figure 1.4(b)). Intellectual realism is also marked by the appearance of simple geometrical shapes, even if the lengths and distances are not always accurate. There is, however, still no Euclidean structuring of spaces.

**Figure 1.4.** *Examples of drawings representing intellectual realism: a) drawing of a duck in its egg; b) drawing without coordination of different points of view [LUQ 27]*

### 1.1.1.3. Stage III: "visual realism"

Visual realism appears, on average, around the age of 8-9 years. This stage is marked not only by the respect of topographical relationships already developed during the intellectual realism stage, but also by the care of respecting perspectives, proportions and lengths in the drawings.

The stage of visual realism highlights three main points:

– that the representation of projection and Euclidean relationships appear after their perception by the child;

– projective relationships do not precede Euclidean ones, nor vice versa, but they are developed simultaneously and nourishing each other;

– children go from step by step constructions induced by the principal use of topographical relationships to constructions of whole bodies, linked to the very nature of projective and Euclidean relationships that conserve positions and distances between figures.

In order to verify their hypotheses and to define the different stages in spatial representation, Piaget and Inhelder developed an experiment that consisted of reproducing the whole or part of a group of 21 models. Table 1.1 is a synopsis of the results and some examples obtained from it.

| Stages and sub-stages | Examples and comments |
|---|---|
| 21 initial shapes suggested to children | |
| Stage 0<br>Up to 2 ½ years old | |
| | Pure scribbles, simple rythmic movements |
| Synthetic incapacity<br>Stage I<br>Sub-stage I A<br>From 2 ½ years to 3 ½ years | <br>Copy of a cross    Copy of a circle<br>Model 21           Model 4 |
| | Distinguished pure scribbles, noticeable distinguishing of open and closed lines. |

| Stages and sub-stages | Examples and comments |
|---|---|
| Synthetic Incapacity Stage I Sub-stage I B From 3 ½ years to 4 years | 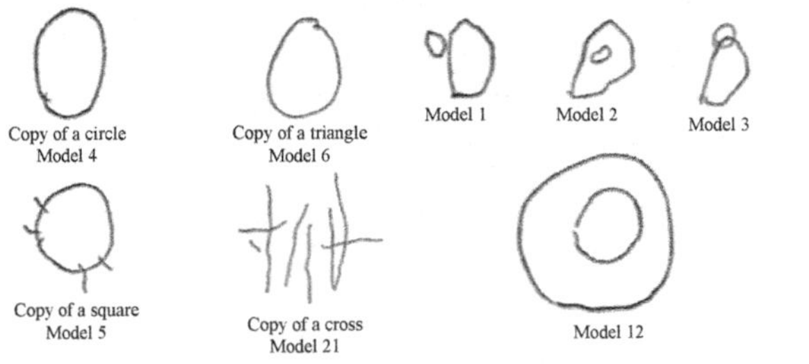 Copy of a circle Model 4   Copy of a triangle Model 6   Model 1   Model 2   Model 3   Copy of a square Model 5   Copy of a cross Model 21   Model 12 |
|  | Topographical relationships are suggested. No distinction between the square, triangle and circle. Distinction between open and closed lines |
| Intellectual realism Stage II Sub-stage II A From 4 to 5 ½ years | 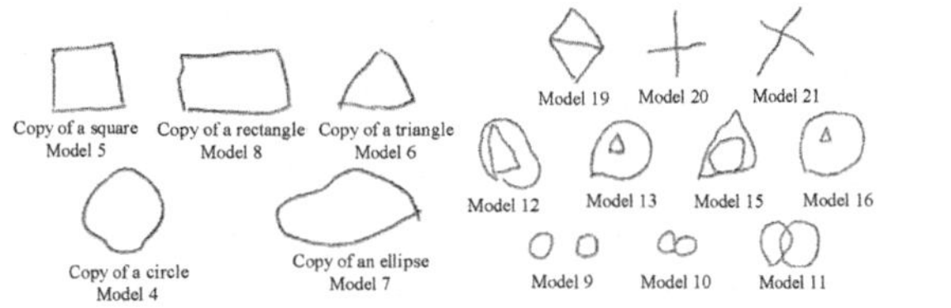 Copy of a square Model 5   Copy of a rectangle Model 8   Copy of a triangle Model 6   Model 19   Model 20   Model 21   Copy of a circle Model 4   Copy of an ellipse Model 7   Model 12   Model 13   Model 15   Model 16   Model 9   Model 10   Model 11 |
|  | Beginning of the distinction of Euclidean shapes. Distinction between rectangular and curved shapes. At the beginning of this stage, there is no distinction between the square and the triangle. |
| Intellectual realism Stage II Sub-stage II B From 5 ½ to 6-7 years | 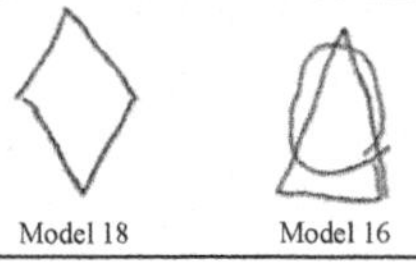 Model 18   Model 16 |
|  | Distinction of Euclidean shapes. Shapes are distinguishable from their angles and dimensions. Figure 16 was not entirely succeeded. |
| Visual realism Stage III From 8-9 years | Children can copy all drawings |

Table 1.1. Synopsis of the development of geometrical representations in children [PIA 48]

## 1.1.2. *Projective space*

According to Piaget, the discovery of the straight line is the simplest manifestation of research into an organization of relationships between objects given projection and coordinate relationships. Indeed, representations of straight lines require the introduction of the understanding that points of the line are hidden from each other (and therefore a certain perspective), or the introduction to lengths and movements along straight lines. Furthermore, even if perceptive recognition of lines can develop early, its representation will not develop until later on. Let us also note that although a line remains a line even when the point of view is changed (the perspective system), for other geometrical shapes such as the circle this is not the case. The experience of constructing a straight line represented by the method of Piaget's aims has shown this discrepancy between recognition of perspective and its representation, linked to the transition from perceptive to representative space.

### 1.1.2.1. *Perspective*

Piaget and Inhelder developed experiments in which children were to do the following:

– first, imagine what shape an object would take when placed in a variety of positions. The two chosen objects are a straight line and a circle, represented by an arrow and a disk, respectively;

– second to represent (or choose depending on the case) two parallel lines representing two rails or the edges of a road. The two parallel lines would normally approach each other due to perspective.

The results of this experiment produced the stages as summarized in Table 1.2. There are three initial stages with several sub-stages. Stage I, synthetic incapacity, is not shown, as children are either unable to represent the required geometric shapes or begin integrating elements from the beginning of stage II, intellectual realism.

### 1.1.2.2. *Developing relationships between perspectives*

As previously discussed, perspectives develop late in children, on average around the age of 9 years, when children are transitioning from intellectual realism to visual realism. It appears that developing perspective requires an overall construction that allows children to create links between several objects simultaneously, as well as from different perspectives, representing the points of view of different observers.

| Stage II: Intellectual realism – Partial or total lack of distinction between different perspectives of the object | |
|---|---|
| Sub-stage II A from 4 to 5 ½ years | Sub-stage II B from 5 ½ to 7 years |
| | |
| Whatever its position, the object is represented with the same shapes and dimensions. | Beginning of distinction of different perspectives. |
| Stage III: Visual realism – Distinction of different perspectives | |
| Sub-stage III A from 7 to 8 ½ - 9 years | Sub-stage III B from 8 ½ - 9 years |
| | |
| Appearance of train tracks on the rails. Remaining difficulties representing limits of the stem or disk. | Systematic appearance of perspective. Objects and rails are represented correctly. |

Table 1.2. *Summary of the development of perspectives in children [PIA 48]*

During his three-mountain experiment, Piaget investigated the representation of perspective of a group of objects, rather than a single one, and studied the relative positions of objects to each other as well as from the point of view of observers in different positions. To carry this out, he constructed a model of three mountains, each of which had a distinct characteristic element as well as a different color (see Figure 1.5), using the following material:

– a wooden doll (without a face so as not to create problems in its direction);

– ten different paintings representing the three mountains from different points of view;

– three cardboard cutouts of the different mountains, in different colors, to be handled.

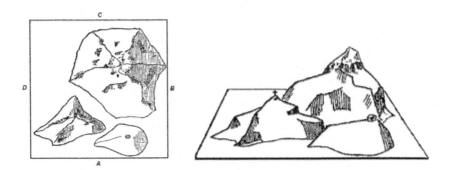

**Figure 1.5.** *Piaget's three mountains. One has a house at its summit, another a cross and the last snow. They are provided in three different colors [PIA 48]. See www.fondationjeanpiaget.ch*

The doll was then placed in different positions represented by the letters A, B, C and D as shown in Figure 1.5. Piaget then asked 100 children between the ages 4 and 12 years to find the corresponding links between the different positions of the doll and the perspectives on the three mountains. In order to gather the answers given by the students, he used three complimentary techniques in his questions:

– he asked the children to construct the scene using three cardboard boxes representing the mountains, then to start the task again but from the wooden doll's point of view, with the child remaining in its initial position;

– the children were shown the ten paintings and asked to choose those which corresponded to the different points of view of the doll in her various positions;

– the children were shown 1 of the 10 paintings and asked to use it to find the position of the doll that would allow her to see the three mountains from this perspective. This task is the opposite to the one described above.

Those children who were in the stage of synthetic incapacity did not understand the questions asked to them and therefore did not participate in this study. For all others, the previously described stages and sub-stages were again noted but with the following characteristics:

– stage II, intellectual realism: children were wholly or partially unable to differentiate between their point of view and that of the doll:

- sub-stage II A: the representation is centered on the child's point of view, whatever the position of the doll, and will be a representation of what he sees,

- sub-stage II B: the representation is still mainly centered on the point of view of the child but shows attempts at distinguishing between his/her perspective and that of the doll. This is a period of transition between the sub-stage II A and stage III;

– stage III, visual realism: children can increasingly distinguish between their point of view and that of the doll:

- sub-stage III A: the concept of the relationship between different points of view is present but incomplete in terms of the number of complex parameters in the scene of the three mountains,

- sub-stage III B: children are capable of determining relative positions of three mountains relative to the different positions of the doll.

After having observed the development of perspective and relationships within them, it is useful to investigate the development of perspectives and projections that will equip children with the skills to create templates, as well as exploring whether this development also follows the previously described stages.

### 1.1.2.3. Nets (folds and surface development)

As illustrated in Figure 1.4(b), during the intellectual realism stage, children naturally use a process that Luquet [LUQ 27] has termed "folding".

In this example, children represent the two wheels and hood of the car in the same plane, naturally using projections. We may then wonder that once a child begins using this process, is he/she also capable of using projections allowing them to develop the lateral surfaces of various solid objects. A summary of these different stages can be found in Table 1.3.

It is interesting to note that children are eventually able to develop lateral surfaces only from the moment where the involuntary folds of intellectual realism have disappeared and they have transitioned into visual realism.

| *Stages* | Stage II: intellectual realism No distinction between different points of view | | Stage III: visual realism Start of correct development | |
|---|---|---|---|---|
| | Sub-stage II A 4 to 5 ½ years | Sub-stage II B 5 ½ to 7 years | Sub-stage III A 7 to 9 years | Sub-stage III B, from 9 years |
| *Cylinder* | | | | Correct representation |
| *Cone* | | | | Correct representation |
| *Cube* | | | | Some remaining difficulties for the cube |
| *Pyramid* | | | | Development not complete for the pyramid |
| *Comments* | The solids, developed or not, are represented in the same way. They are represented by one of their characteristics. | Beginning of distinction between developed and non-developed solids. | Marks of a phase of the development, but no wholly complete results | Representations of the development of the cube and pyramid are only shown from age 11-12 years onward |

**Table 1.3.** *Summary of the development of surface representations in children. There are two types of representation: a) profile view; b) lateral surface development [PIA 48]*

### 1.1.3. *Euclidean space*

Whether from an axiomatic point of view or that of the development of representation of space in children, projective and Euclidean space are linked by two types of relations:

– both ensue from the topographical space;

– the affinities and similarities form a passage between these two spaces.

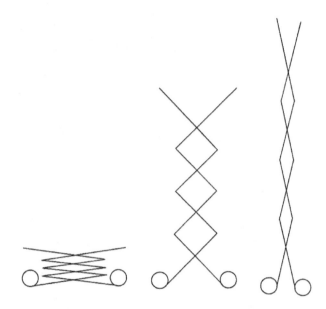

**Figure 1.6.** *Affine transformations of lozenges: "Nuremberg's scissors" [PIA 48]. See www.fondationjeanpiaget.ch*

As previously explained, the projective and Euclidean spaces are developed simultaneously and in parallel, with the development of one nourishing the development of the other. All of the aforementioned stages are also present in these developments. Table 1.4 summarizes the results from the "Nuremburg's scissors" experiment (see Figure 1.6), where children were asked to anticipate and draw what would take place when the scissors were opened. This experience focused on the affine transformations of lozenges as well as the conservation of parallelism.

| Stages | Examples and comments |
|---|---|
| Intellectual realism<br>Stage II<br>Sub-stage II A<br>From 4 to 5 ½ years | |
| | Absence of any recognition of the lozenges in the overall structure, where they are represented by crosses. Subsequently, children remain unable to draw the lozenges correctly. |
| Intellectual realism<br>Stage II<br>Sub-stage II B<br>From 5 ½ to 7 years | |
| | Awareness and the ability to anticipate the modifications has grown but this is translated by a change in the lengths of the sides rather than by conservation of parallelism. |
| Visual realism<br>Stage III<br>Sub-stage III A<br>From 7 to 9-10 years | |
| | Correct structuration of the lozenges with lengths remaining consistent and parallelism conserved, but with difficulties remaining in the relationships used for construction |
| Visual realism<br>Stage III<br>Sub-stage II B<br>From 9-10 years | Explicit formulation of the relationships used in construction. |

**Table 1.4.** *Summary of the results obtained from the "Nuremburg's scissors" experiment [PIA 48]*

## 1.1.4. Summary

After having studied topographical relationships, drawings of geometrical shapes, their perspectives and their relationships to one another as well as the development of the lateral surfaces of solids, we have found that the three initially suggested stages allow us to structure the development of spatial perspective in children. From these three stages, which are synthetic incapacity, intellectual realism and visual realism, we have found that the group of elements necessary to understand solid shapes, including polyhedrons, is only developed from the stage of visual realism. In the case of patterns, this development takes place even later – in sub-stage III B that begins from the age of 9. This is why in the study to follow we will focus on school children aged at least 9 years.

## 1.2. The representation of geometric objects: the status of drawings

In his studies on spatial representation in children, Piaget [PIA 48] based his work upon the findings of Luquet [LUQ 27] on children's drawings. We may note that in the different drawings explained previously, the children were asked to draw these shapes freehand and without the use of a ruler in order to avoid added motor difficulties for the younger participants. In mathematics, we often hear of figures, drawings, representations and geometrical objects. It is necessary to clarify these terms before continuing any further.

### 1.2.1. *Status of drawings in mathematics: drawings versus figures*

Many didactics have studied the differences between figures, drawings and mathematic or geometric objects. Arsac [ARS 89] distinguishes between figures and sketches through their origins in the "mathematical world" and the "tangible world", respectively:

> "From now on we shall distinguish between drawings and figures by naming the drawing as the drawing carried out on a sheet of paper (or, in the case of Archimedes, in the sand) and the figure as the mathematical object of which the drawing is but a representation... as such, the figure is an element belonging to the "mathematical world" rather than the tangible one".

Parzysz [PAR 88, PAR 89] distinguishes between a figure that corresponds to a theoretical geometrical object and a drawing that is simply a representation among all those possible. In 1994, Laborde and Capponi [LAB 94] refined this difference:

> "As a material entity on a support, the drawing may be considered as a signifier of a theoretical reference (the object of a geometrical theory such as Euclidean or projective geometry). A geometrical figure is the matching of a given reference in all of its drawings and is as such defined as the set of all couples made up of two terms, the first being the reference and the second being one of the drawings that represents it; this second term refers to all possible drawings of the reference. In

this context, the term "geometrical figure" refers to the development of a relationship between a geometrical object and its possible representations. Using this approach, the relationships constructed by the subject as either the reader or creator of the sketch, between this drawing and its reference form the meaning of the geometrical figure for the subject".

These distinctions between figure and drawing seem to be complimentary. Indeed, the work required of students during primary and secondary 3D geometry learning refers to three main objects:

– physical objects from the tangible world suggested by Arsac [ARS 89];

– geometrical objects considered as such to be mathematical objects attached to a theory;

– drawings that are representations of either the physical or geometrical objects.

Chaachoua [CHA 97] suggests a diagram that outlines the relationships between these three types of objects (see Figure 1.7). It also outlines the three different statuses of drawings in the teaching of geometry:

– drawings as physical objects: in this case, it is considered as the point of study;

– drawings as models of a geometrical shape: in this case, it is considered as the signifier of a theoretical reference as suggested by Laborde and Capponi [LAB 94];

– drawings as models of a physical shape, as is particularly the case in primary education where the representation of solid objects leads to the development of axes (1), (2) and (3) of Figure 1.7.

In the case of 3D geometry, there are more difficulties than in the case of planar geometry. Indeed, students have to be able to represent 3D shapes with 2D sketches, generally carried out on paper. In this case, the representation of 3D geometrical shapes can only be carried out using projections, thus leading to the loss of information. It then becomes necessary to represent them using codes that enable students to both carry out and interpret these representations. Bkouche [BKO 83] suggests the following:

"3D scenes appear through representations that transform them into planar figures, thus requiring a code, both for the reading and writing of this transformation... In this case, learning about 3D geometry through the mediation of planar representation does not build on observations as in the case of planar geometry, and therefore it is impossible to reflect upon a figure that is already distinct from the *reality* it is supposed to represent. This type of thinking will therefore require the development of a set of complex reasoning" etc.

The following sections will develop some different possibilities for representing 3D geometrical shapes.

In this context, Chaachoua [CHA 97] suggests an adaptation of his diagram that links physical and geometrical shapes to drawings (see Figure 1.7) in order to take into account the added complexity of 3D geometry (see Figure 1.8).

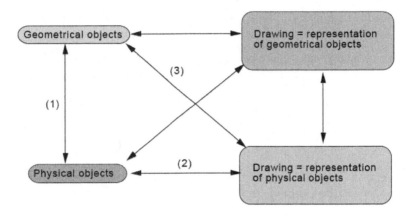

**Figure 1.7.** *Representation of the relationships between physical objects, geometrical objects and sketches [CHA 97]*

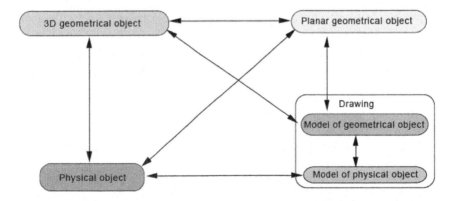

**Figure 1.8.** *Representation of the relationships between physical and geometrical shapes and sketches in the context of 3D geometry [CHA 97]*

After having clarified the differences and the links between figures and drawings, we will discuss the use of geometrical representations, in particular in 3D geometry.

### 1.2.2. *Use of geometrical representations*

Throughout a child's education, especially throughout primary and middle school, the use of representations in geometry evolves. As such, students will use the following three types of geometry:

– perceptive geometry in which the simple fact of observing something on a sketch in enough to justify any assertions (it is a lozenge because I see it);

– instrumental geometry in which the use of instruments allows the justification of the reasoning (it is a lozenge because I measured the four sides and they are all the same length);

– deductive geometry in which students use the characteristics of figures throughout proofs in order to show a result (it is a lozenge because the diagonals cross in their midpoints and are perpendicular).

As Parzysz [PAR 06] explains, the transition between these different types of geometry is often the source of error for students:

"[...] although [representation] constitutes a useful aide in conjectures, it can equally become an obstacle to surmount in proofs as the "proof of the figure" can be the source of confusion in the use of facts".

In this context, the geometrical paradigms of Houdemont and Kuzniak [HOU 06] as well as Duval's [DUV 05] cognitive approach will be discussed.

#### 1.2.2.1. *The three geometrical paradigms of Houdemont and Kuzniak*

Houdemont and Kuzniak [HOU 06] established three geometrical paradigms:

– natural geometry;

– natural axiomatic geometry;

– axiomatic geometry

##### 1.2.2.1.1. Natural geometry (GI)

Natural geometry (GI) is based first on a real model. Its validation is based on confrontation with the tangible or physical world. It is, therefore, principally based on perception and the use of geometrical instruments on shapes. Mithalal [MIT 10] agrees with Balacheff [BAL 99] who considers that "it is possible to substitute material actions in GI for immaterial ones, a mental process in which the reference to the material action is no less present".

Natural geometry encompasses perceptive and instrumental geometry and falls under teaching of the period of primary to the beginning of secondary education. Within it, there is no formalization of geometric shapes so to speak nor do proofs have much purpose as it is mainly based on drawings rather than figures.

### 1.2.2.1.2. Natural axiomatic geometry (GII)

Natural axiomatic geometry (GII) is based on an axiomatic system. Here, validation is based on the mathematical properties of the shape as well as both hypothetical and deductive laws. This type of geometry is "natural" in the sense that it remains attached to a reference based in reality, as opposed to a purely formal geometric one. Its axiom also aims to model 3D problems, constraining it to the domain of Euclidean geometry.

Natural axiomatic geometry encompasses deductive geometry studied during secondary education.

### 1.2.2.1.3. Axiomatic geometry (GIII)

Axiomatic geometry (GIII) is solely based on axioms where their validity relies on non-contradiction. It is detached from reality and encompasses, for example, non-Euclidean or projective geometry. As it is totally absent from both primary and secondary education, it will not be covered here any further.

### 1.2.2.1.4. Explanation of the different paradigms

As previously stated, both GI and GII make up primary and secondary education. So although at some points students will be further within one of these paradigms, they do not pass instantly from one into the other. In order to take into account the explanation between these different geometries and shifts, even the back and forth between them, Houdemont and Kuzniak [HOU 06] (see Figure 1.9) and, later on, Kuzniak [KUZ 06] developed the notion of geometrical workspace (ETG):

"We have more accurately [KUZ 03, KUZ 04], named as geometrical workspace, the area organized by the geometer for the use of the network that makes up the three poles, the material support that is the real and local space, the group of artifacts will be the tools and instruments at their disposition, and finally the theoretical reference to be organized into a theoretical model that will depend on the chosen geometry. The workspace only begins to make sense and become useful and operational when it is possible to use the relationship of the three poles previously outlined".

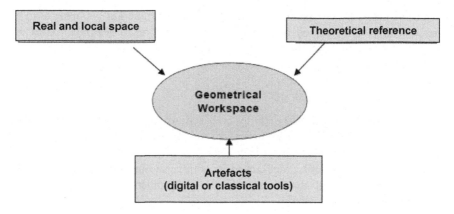

**Figure 1.9.** *Diagram showing the geometrical workspace [HOU 06]*

After having studied the geometrical paradigms of Houdemont and Kuzniak [HOU 06], we will now study Duval's [DUV 05] more cognitive approach, which has itself led to the evolving of the geometrical workspace diagram.

*1.2.2.2. Duval's cognitive point of view*

Although we are often unaware of it, the act of "seeing" involves the implementation of two complimentary but independent processes. The first of these is *"the discriminative recognition of shapes"* and the second *"the identification of known shapes"* [DUV 05]. So even if these two operations seem to be simultaneous in everyday life, this is not the case when confronted with outline-constructed representations:

"However, this does not apply to the perception of representations made up of outlines in drawings. There is no intrinsic relationship between the recognized shapes in the outline and the shape that the outline is "supposed" to represent. How then does one carry out the transition from one to the other? This passage is based on a "similarity" between the visually discriminative shape and the typical form of the shape represented" [DUV 05].

Figure 1.10 illustrates Duval's words. Indeed, to the left, we will immediately recognize a cube, more particularly a Rubik's cube, whereas on the right a cube in isometric perspective is shown, and can also be seen as the assembly of three lozenges.

Duval put forward two opposing modes of cognitive function in the visualization of geometry: iconic visualization and non-iconic visualization [DUV 05].

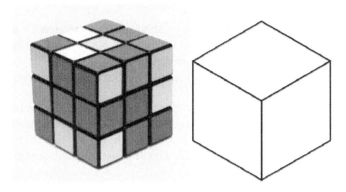

**Figure 1.10.** *On the left, a Rubik's cube in the shape of a cube and on the right a cube in isometric perspective that can be seen as an assembly of three lozenges*

### 1.2.2.2.1. Iconic visualization

In the case of iconic visualization, the identification operation is based on the similarity between the recognized representation and a reference from the point of view of the object. In this context, the shape is seen above all as a stable outline that cannot be transformed. Here, the studied object is the drawing and belongs to GI-type geometry. From Duval:

> "The main tendencies of iconic visualization go against the development of what must become the first reflex in geometry: taking apart all shapes whether recognized as a group of outlines or as a random starting shape, into a configuration of other figural units with the same or a smaller number of dimensions" [DUV 05]

### 1.2.2.2.2. Non-iconic visualization

In the case of non-iconic visualization, shapes can be decomposed into elementary compositions called *figural units* that can be assembled to form figures. Depending on the context, points, segments or even polygons can be figural units.

For example, in a rectangle, the segments representing its sides are figural units and for these segments its points are figural units. In this context, Duval describes the *deconstruction* of shapes whose aim is the exact opposite, that is to carry out a *reconstruction*:

> "In other words, the activity of construction of figures [... ] is based on the deconstruction of their outlines [. . . ]. *All the attention of this deconstruction lies in the reconstruction* [... ]" [DUL 05].

So, in order to construct a figure, we must be able to deconstruct it mentally, that is to break it up into *figural units* or to find the plan of its construction (and chronology). In order to carry out these deconstructions, Duval [DUV 05] developed two types of procedures: the addition of ancillary and of reorganizational outlines.

The addition of ancillary outlines consists of the appearance or rediscovery of outlines that may have been used during construction of the drawing, which in this context is seen as a chain of temporary actions (see Figure 1.11). The addition of ancillary outlines is therefore associated with the instrumental deconstruction that Mithalal [MIT 10] defines as follows:

> "We will define an instrumental decomposition of a shape as the identification of a group of independent figural units, the *primitives*, and of the succession of actions carried out thanks to the use of instruments, allowing the reconstruction of the shape itself or of its graphical representation".

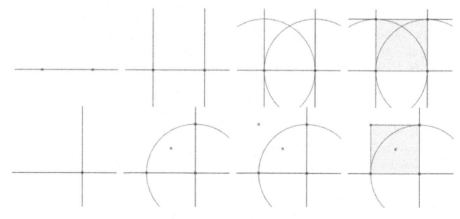

**Figure 1.11.** *Two instrumental deconstructions of a square, as suggested by Mithalal [MIT 10]*

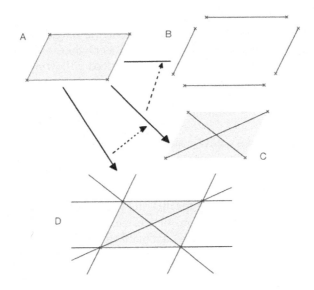

**Figure 1.12.** *Decomposition into figural units by dimensional deconstruction of a parallelogram: a) from its side (b); its diagonals (c); from a group of outlines (d); [DUV 05]*

The addition of reorganizational outlines corresponds to dimensional deconstruction that is based on the decomposition of the representation of a group of figural units of fewer dimensions and of whom the coherence is assured based on relationships (see Figure 1.12). Mithalal [MIT 10] defines this dimensional deconstruction as follows:

> "We will define dimensional deconstruction of a shape as the following pair ({figural units},{relations}). To carry out this operation on a drawing is to attach it to such a pair ({figural units},{relations}) of which it can be a representative. To carry this out on a figure is to determine such a pair that will allow for a description of the figure itself".

Note that the same figure can be represented by several different dimensional deconstructions as described by Mithalal [MIT 10].

### 1.2.2.2.3. Dimensional hiatus

By basing his work on non-iconic visualization and dimensional deconstruction, Duval [DUV 05] showed the hiatus that opposes the "normal" visualization mode and "formal" language [DUV 05]. Indeed, the "normal" mode of visualization "tends to fuse together the *figural units of lower rank* INTO A SINGLE FIGURAL UNIT OF HIGHER RANK". The "formal" geometric language, on the contrary, tends to consider the dimensional deconstruction as obvious and, as such, from an educational point of view, knowledge is introduced following progress that is seemingly organized as follows:

((((points→ lines)→ segments of lines)→ polygons) →polyhedrons)

Figure 1.13 illustrates this contradiction that Duval calls "cognitively paralyzing". In order to facilitate the understanding of this figure, Mithalal's definition is introduced:

"We will name "figural unit nD/mD" the figural unit of dimension n, submerged in a space of m dimensions. For example, a point represented in the plane will be a figural unit 0D/2D. A segment, a figural unit 1D/2D if it is planar, or 1D/3D if it is represented in 3D" [MIT 10].

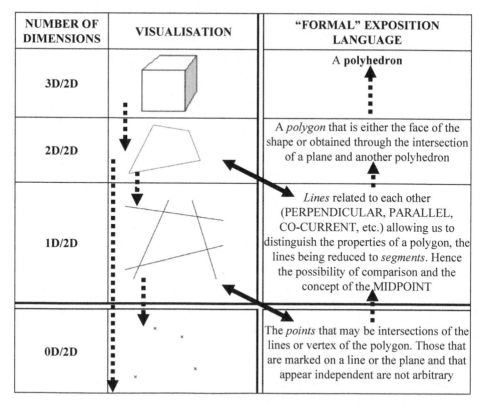

| NUMBER OF DIMENSIONS | VISUALISATION | "FORMAL" EXPOSITION LANGUAGE |
|---|---|---|
| 3D/2D | | A **polyhedron** |
| 2D/2D | | A *polygon* that is either the face of the shape or obtained through the intersection of a plane and another polyhedron |
| 1D/2D | | *Lines* related to each other (PERPENDICULAR, PARALLEL, CO-CURRENT, etc.) allowing us to distinguish the properties of a polygon, the lines being reduced to *segments*. Hence the possibility of comparison and the concept of the MIDPOINT |
| 0D/2D | | The *points* that may be intersections of the lines or vertex of the polygon. Those that are marked on a line or the plane and that appear independent are not arbitrary |

**Figure 1.13.** *Dimensional hiatus [DUV 05]*

## 1.2.3. *The three main functions of drawings in geometry*

Basing his work on Duval, Houdemont-Kuzniak and Chaachoua's theories, Mithalal proposed the following three functions of drawings:

> "In the end, one must retain three main functions of the drawing, independently from the concept of the activity from which it originates:
>
> – an illustrative function, used to illustrate a statement, problem, stages of reasoning or a response to a problem;
>
> – a hypoth*esis organization function*, translated as the capacity of drawings to show information that may be absent in the geometrical shapes;
>
> – an *experimentation function*, which depends on the illustrative function but also on the interpretive domain of drawings" [MIT 10].

It, therefore, appears that drawings, as suspected, are omnipresent in geometry during primary and secondary teaching, whether this is in the case of perceptive, instrumental or deductive geometry. Mithalal [MIT 10] considers that "seeing" in geometry corresponds to the capacity to link representations to the three functions explained above.

However, if these functions are easily used in planar geometry, they can become a problem for students in the case of 3D geometry, as explained by Mithalal:

> "'seeing in 3D' can be a problem: for students who can no longer use drawings as a reasoning tool as well as for teachers who lose its illustrative function" [MIT 10].

Confronted with this problem of spatial visualization and of the planar representation of 3D shapes, we shall explain the transition between the physical object and its planar representation during primary and secondary schooling.

## 1.3. From the physical shape to its planar representation

### 1.3.1. *The institutional perspective*

As we have seen so far, many obstacles present themselves during the learning of geometry in general and in particular for 3D geometry. After having clarified the development of spatial representations in children as well as the status of drawings versus figures in geometry, we will now see how these concepts are tackled institutionally and with regard to curriculums throughout French primary and secondary schools.

### 1.3.1.1. Primary

Table 1.5 summarizes the 3D geometry knowledge and competencies required from students throughout primary school.

| Class | Required knowledge and competencies |
|-------|-------------------------------------|
| CP | – To recognize and name the cube and cuboid. |
| CE1 | – To know and use an appropriate elementary geometrical vocabulary. <br> – To recognize, describe and name some rectangular solids: cube, cuboid. |
| CE2 | – To recognize, describe and name: cubes and cuboids. <br> – To use the vocabulary: surface, edges, vertices. |
| CM1 | – To recognize, describe and name right-angle solids: cube, cuboid, prism. <br> – To recognize or complete nets of cubes or cuboids. |
| CM2 | – To recognize, describe and name right-angle solids: cube, cuboid, cylinder, prism. <br> – To recognize or complete nets of cuboids. |

**Table 1.5.** *Summary of the primary curriculums for 3D learning*

It is interesting to note that institutional documents referring to spatial structuring contain Piaget's three mountains experiment as the task to be given to children to practise decentering competencies. It is important to note that these documents also underline the fact that 15-year-old students still have substantial difficulties with the representation of 3D shapes in perspective.

We shall note that we are now referring to GI-type geometry. The accompanying documents explain that the competencies linked to deductive reasoning are only developed during secondary education and that it is therefore at this point a true shift between the GI and GII types of geometry.

We shall now study the secondary curriculum as we just have for the primary school curriculum.

### 1.3.1.2. *Secondary*

The 2008 secondary curricula are based on a continuity of those from the primary education. Although there is an accompanying document referring to geometry, it only very briefly references 3D geometry to state that (unlike with the beginning of deductive planar reasoning): "the study of 3D objects continues as essentially experimental during middle school".

Without going into the details of what is required in secondary education, the main objectives are as follows:

– transitioning between perceptive identification of shapes and configurations (recognizing by sight) and characterization of them using their properties (transition between drawings and figures);

– isolating, in a given configuration, the elements required to answer a question;

– familiarization with spatial representations, in particular the use of the usual conventions for the allowed process for these representations;

– discovering some simple geometric transformations: symmetries – axial and central symmetries;

– developing a directory of theorems and learning to use them.

### 1.3.1.3. *Summary of secondary curriculums*

It is interesting to note that several elements either do not change from primary school or appear in curricula from 2008. As such, we may note that for each year in middle school, the learning objectives for 3D geometry are stated as being the natural continuation of the familiarization of students with planar representations of 3D objects. On the one hand, this underlines the stated difficulties of passing from a physical object to its planar representation, and on the other shows that geometry teaching remains of the GI type, as in primary school. We may therefore study the implementation of the teaching of 3D geometry throughout primary and secondary education. It seems to be essential that students are able to pass through the transition of a solid to its representation. Incidentally, the use of 3D geometry programs appears for the first time in secondary curricula.

### 1.3.2. *Teaching 3D geometry*

Although it may seem obvious that the ability to manipulate physical objects and solid shapes is essential, it is necessary but insufficient as a condition. From the curricula of the first year of secondary education, the required knowledge is associated with the representation of a rectangular shape in perspective. It is interesting to note that in order to acquire details of the nature of representation in perspective, we must search the comments column. This therefore allows for the opportunity to study, first of all, several representations in perspective in order to choose the most useful one. We shall study this point further on in the book. Furthermore, although the term "perspective" does not appear in primary school level curriculums, it is widely used in its school books (see Figure 1.14).

To quote Bonafé and Sauter [BON 98] on the importance of a rapid development of spatial representation during middle school:

"Teaching 3D geometry may have chances of succeeding, only if from the first few years of middle school, a process for representing 3D shapes is put into place, alongside the required skills and learning. To gain awareness of the geometrical differences between an object and its representations is also crucial, as a student will be unable to work with the drawing of a shape unless they have a sufficiently good mental image of the object as well as a perfect understanding of the rules of representation that will allow it to decode the drawing".

In this context, Bonafé and Sauter suggest adopting an identical approach to study all shapes [BON 98]. This approach can be split into two large parts that we will briefly explain:

– manipulation of objects;

– learn how to represent objects.

Bonafé and Sauter prescribe beginning the study of an object systematically and by using everyday objects as well as models built by the students using nets provided by the teacher. The use of models made by the students as well as everyday objects allows the development of the required vocabulary on a solid visual reference of the object. Furthermore, the models that each student will build can be used from then on as a reference.

The authors next study the representation of solid shapes. They suggest beginning with a situation that will allow the comparison of physical solids from the tangible world in order to highlight any properties that are modified or conserved during the transition into planar representation.

Finally, they put forward three main elements that seem to allow students to develop good mental images:

– the transition from object to drawing;

– the transition from drawing to object: the student must reconstruct an object from its representation;

– the transition from drawing to drawing without any object: the student must pass from one representation of an object to another, based only on their mental image of the object.

Starting from the approach recommended by Bonafé and Sauter [BON 98], we can propose one that will cover the whole of primary and secondary education, while adding several elements that seem important. The transition of these 3D objects into their planar representation thereby happens progressively; so, we suggest the following approach:

– observation and manipulation of physical solids;

– making solid models;

– studying pictures of shapes in order to highlight the first rules of planar representation from a situation that makes sense to students;

– carrying out the first representations;

– confrontation between a solid and its first representation;

– repetition of Bonafé and Sauter's elements.

Until now, we have covered the planar representations of 3D objects, particularly representations in perspective, without necessarily going into detail about the different types of representation. Outside the development that we have suggested here, the representation given by photography and oblique projections is different. We shall now detail the different types of representation, at least those that are most common in teaching, in order to list the possible choices and the justification for each of them.

### 1.3.3. *Different representations of 3D objects*

As we have previously seen in Bonafé and Sauter's [BON 98] suggested development, two big types of representations exist for 3D objects:

– models;

– planar representations.

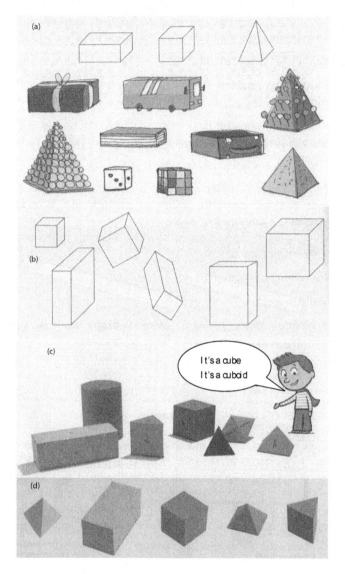

**Figure 1.14.** *Representations in perspective used by primary education:*
*a) La Tribu des maths CP (year 1); b) Maths+ CP (year 1);*
*c) Cap Maths CE1 (year 2); d) Cap Maths CE2 (year 2)*

### 1.3.3.1. *Models*

Models are the first method of representing 3D objects that students are likely to learn about. From primary school, students are confronted with this type of representation, the first traces of which were found institutionally in the 19th Century. Here, it can be used interchangeably as well as of belonging to the tangible world along with 3D objects. Furthermore, the choice of the type of model will highlight different elements of the 3D object, such as edges and faces. Indeed, throughout primary schools, we may find different types of models, made of paper or rigid rods to highlight the edges and vertices, even from polydrons© for studying faces or foam blocks for studying whole shapes (see Figure 1.15). It is not the possibility but the first elements that will later allow students to develop a non-iconic vision.

As stated by Grenier and Tanguay [GRE 08], many didactic studies have highlighted the importance of the use of these models in the teaching of 3D geometry:

> "Most didactic studies on 3D geometry [...] highlight that the importance of the development of the "spatial awareness" must, in order to be effective, go through a phase of work (construction, manipulation, observation, description, etc.) using *tridimensional models that can be handled* of 3D geometrical shapes".

By always referring back to the previously outlined developments, the transition between the 3D representation of the tangible world and the planar representation of the 3D object must be successful (and is where the difficulty lies).

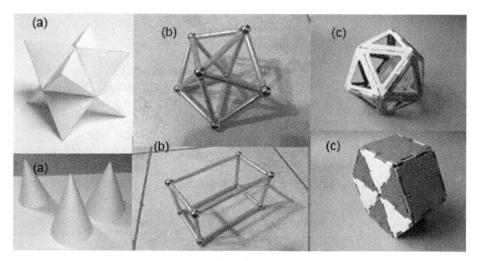

**Figure 1.15.** *Different types of models found in primary and secondary school: a) paperboard; b) rigid rods; c) Polydron©*

### 1.3.3.2. *Planar representations of 3D objects*

When the student (and/or the teacher) goes from a tridimensional to a planar representation, the question of which planar representation to use is posed. The transition into the plane generally takes place through the use of projections, thus implicating many representational possibilities such as central perspective, cavalier projection, isometric or spherical perspectives, the four views of a technical drawing, (see Figure 1.16).

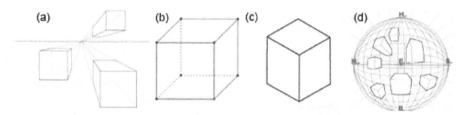

**Figure 1.16.** *Different types of representations in perspective:*
*a) central perspective; b) cavalier projection;*
*c) isometric perspective; d) spherical perspective*

Here, only two of the types of perspective used in current teaching methods will be covered: central perspective (also known as linear or conical perspective) and cavalier projections.

### 1.3.3.2.1. Central perspective

Central perspective is no doubt the closest method of representation to human vision. Indeed, it is similar to photographs. Lismont and Rouche [LIS 99] defined representations in central perspective as the use of an image as follows:

"Central perspective is reproducing on paper what the eye (unmoving and punctual) would see through a 'window'. The idea is that if the paper were to take the place of the window, the eye would be unable to tell the difference ... This type of representation has the following characteristics":

– assuming that the eye is a point;

– each point of the represented object is linked to the eye through a straight visual beam;

– each point of the representation is the intersection of this beam with the paper".

In the context of the previous development of the teaching of 3D geometry, central perspective therefore belongs fully to the study of objects from pictures, at least at the beginning. Comparing this representation in perspective with a picture poses no difficulty; however, the comparison with physical objects from the tangible world highlights its main defect, which is that it does not respect mathematical properties. Indeed, in this perspective, lines that are parallel in reality may not be here – midpoints do not always remain in the middle.

In order to be able to reason, at least partially, based on one of these figures, and to conserve some minimal mathematical properties, it is essential to use another type of perspective.

## 1.3.3.2.2. Cavalier projections

Although any type of planar representation of a 3D object will lead to some degree of loss of information, we must still choose the most appropriate planar representation for teaching 3D geometry. Audibert and Keita [AUD 87] state that it must be cavalier projections:

> "And AUDIBERT G. (1985) suggests the following hypothesis: the student needs perspective; cavalier projections are the most satisfactory".

Cavalier projections are well adapted to the task because they use rules of drawing that have already been assimilated by children. Indeed, Dolle [DOL 80], Audibert [AUD 85], followed then by Audibert and Bonafé [AUD 87] put forward the importance and advantages of these rules:

> "[...] the verticals remain vertical, and they note [the authors] that this criterion is taken into account at the age of 11. [...] The second rule that is unanimous in our students is that of the conservation of the midpoint [...]. The third is admitted naturally: the foremost face, parallel to the plane in which the drawing is being carried out, is represented in real dimensions. [...] The ease with which these three rules are listed by our students reinforces the idea that cavalier projection (CP) is an appropriate tool" [AUD 87].

The conservation of parallelism can be added to these three rules and is put forward in the definition of Bautier *et al.* [BAU 87]:

> "Cavalier projection is a method of parallel projection determined by a plane, D, and the direction of a line d, non-parallel to D (direction of the projections). The image of a point M in the space is the point m, the intersection of the line of direction d, passing through M with the plane D; all points in space have an image.

"Cavalier projections are affine transformations; such that they conserve the midpoints of segments, parallelism of lines and relationships of length for parallel segments; all these properties are easy to use in constructing drawings".

Parzysz [PAR 91] considers cavalier perspective to be a representation that will allow the transfer of properties and through this create an equilibrium between what is seen and what is known by the student:

"The reason for this choice when it comes to geometrical drawings, other than the ease of execution, must be in the fact that parallel perspective allows for an acceptable compromise between seeing and knowing (transfer of proprieties)".

Although all these different justifications of the use of cavalier perspective employ terms such as "naturally", "easy" and "ease", this type of representation is far from easy for students. Indeed, Keita [KEI 86] puts forward the fact that 70% of the first year University students do not respect the rules of cavalier perspective. Following this, Audibert and Keita [AUD 87] highlighted the difficulties in carrying out and interpreting cavalier perspective drawings by students (see Figure 1.17).

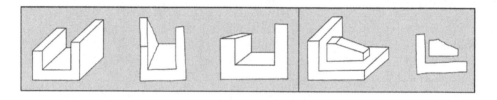

**Figure 1.17.** *Two student productions of the front view from a view in perspective [AUD 87]*

### 1.3.4. *The conflict between the SEEN and the KNOWN in children*

Previously cavalier perspective was described by Parzysz as "an acceptable compromise between the seen and the known". Without questioning the work of Piaget, Colmez and Parzysz [COL 93] suggested a slightly different model based on the position of the student productions relative to two opposite poles:

– the SEEN: pole in which the student will represent the object depending on its imagined visualization;

– the KNOWN: pole in which the student will represent the object depending on the properties that it thinks to be important.

The student then navigates between these two poles through a necessary compromise to arrive at the representation it thinks best. These compromises evolve depending on different elements such as age (linking up with Piaget's model), geometrical knowledge or even the type of exercise given.

During their studies, Colmez and Parzysz analyzed 1,500 drawings from over 1,200 students aged between 8 and 17 years. They were then able to regroup them into 21 categories that were then divided into two families of drawings (see Figure 1.18). The first of these groups is those that put forward an edge, whereas the second one is those that put forward a face.

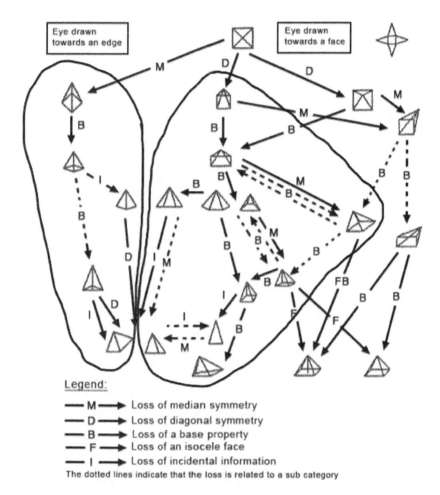

Legend:
— M ➤ Loss of median symmetry
— D ➤ Loss of diagonal symmetry
— B ➤ Loss of a base property
— F ➤ Loss of an isocele face
— I ➤ Loss of incidental information
The dotted lines indicate that the loss is related to a sub category

**Figure 1.18.** *Diagram showing the organization of the categories relative to KNOWING [COL 93]*

The analysis of students' drawings allowed them to highlight two main types of proceedings. The first relates to the drawings that have been carried out based on a lateral face, and the second relates to the drawings that were carried out from the point of view of the base (see Figure 1.19). This allows us to note that the KNOWN is omnipresent, whether through the drawing of a truly square base or a lateral face represented by an isosceles triangle, or even the representation of the altitude of a pyramid.

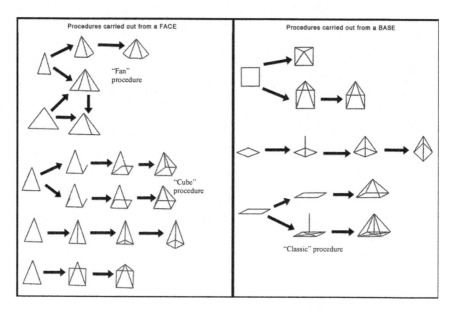

**Figure 1.19.** *Procedures carried out from:*
*a) a FACE; b) a BASE [COL 93]*

Their studies highlighted three different stages:

– from CE2 to CM (Year 4 to 6, between 8 and 10 years old), drawings in perspective are carried out based on what is SEEN;

– from CM to 3ème (Year 5 to 10, between 10 and 15 years old), there is a conflict between what is SEEN and what is KNOWN;

– from 3ème (Year 10 or the age of 15), drawings in perspective are based on what is KNOWN, and are therefore based on reasoning alone.

As in Piaget's model, the transitions between these three stages are not immediate and students pass progressively through these one by one, sometimes returning backward and forward between them.

In order to resolve this mental conflict between solids and their planar representation, Audibert and Bonafé [AUD 86] strongly suggest the use of real solids or their construction by students. They highlight the importance of manipulations that will show the contradictions between a solid and its representation.

All of the elements described since the beginning of this chapter allow us to justify our choice of studied age range. First, from the studies of Piaget and other didacticians, the necessary elements to a successful transition between the object and its planar representation are only present from the age of 9 years. Second, from the age of 15, problems between the SEEN and the KNOWN seem to lessen, at least for the vast majority of students. We will therefore set our age range at 9-15 years.

As previously explained, in secondary curricula, the use of dynamic 3D geometry programs is highly advocated by the institution. We shall now analyze the advantages and disadvantages linked to the use of such programs. We shall also study the innovative technologies that, despite not being explicitly advocated in curricula yet, have been shown by several studies to have educational benefits.

## 1.4. Benefits of new technologies and dynamic 3D geometry

Many dynamic planar geometry programs exist such as Geoplan, Geonext, MathGraph32, Cabri-géomètre, Tracenpoche, CaRMetal or even GeoGebra that is no doubt the most widely known and used. On the contrary, programs relating to 3D geometry are much more rare. Those that can be listed are Geospace, Calque 3D, Série3D and Cabri-3D (see Figure 1.20).

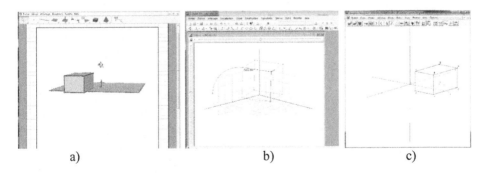

a)                                    b)                                    c)

**Figure 1.20.** *Three different dynamic 3D geometry programs:*
*a) Cabri 3D; b) Calque 3D; c) Geospace*

The use of these dynamic geometry and particularly 3D geometry programs is an important part of curricula, at least during secondary school. We may even wonder why such recommendations are absent from the curricula in cycle 3 of primary school. Indeed, in cases where the use of such programs would be of educational benefit, it would allow for a continuous path between primary and secondary education by facilitating the transition between tangible solids and their representation, already heavily used in school books (see Figure 1.14).

The first question to ask is: what is the benefit of such programs in 3D geometry?

The second is: what part must "technology" play in these possible benefits?

### 1.4.1. *Advantages of 3D geometry programs*

As highlighted by Osta [OST 87], the introduction of IT in schools was debated and gave rise to many questions on the potential benefits it could offer (at the time of computers). In his study, he considered computers as a tool to help in teaching rather than as an object of study in itself. He particularly studied the role of the computer as a facilitator in the transition from physical space to graphic planar representation. According to Osta [OST 87], digital tools bring a new dimension to 3D geometrical learning situations thanks to "dynamic data treatment" that allows us to leave behind the static nature of drawings:

> "Drawings are no longer a static support for the representation of an object, but rather belong to the heart of the problem and so it is through the drawing that the students conception of it will manifest and evolve" [OST 87].

However, even if Osta's study showed that the use of technology in a teaching sequence is possible from a conceptual and educational theory point of view, it does not verify the results obtained through a situational check of the sequence.

More recent studies, such as those of Chaachoua [CHA 97], followed by Mithalal [MIT 10], confirmed elements sensed by Osta in 1987. In his doctoral thesis, Chaachoua [CHA 97] puts forward limitations in the interpretation of the drawing of a 3D geometrical object in a "paper–pencil" environment:

> "[…] we have shown that the domain of interpretation of a drawing, the model of a 3D geometrical object, is very reduced, and functions following different rules from those of drawing, model of a planar geometrical object".

After having carried out his studies based on two 3D geometry programs (Geospace and Cabri 3D), Chaachoua [CHA 97] came to the conclusion that the technological environment increases the size of the field of drawing:

"[...] the technological environment can increase the size of the experimental field of sketches, models of a planar or 3D geometric object" [CHA 97].

Mithalal [MIT 10], evaluated technological benefits based on the different functions of drawings (see section 2.3) and using the program Cabri-3D. In the context of a technological environment, Mithalal notes a "better illustrative function" essentially linked to a decrease in complexity of the perceptive examination, allowing technology to fill a space by positioning itself between the model and its paper representation:

"This decrease in complexity is a major advantage of digital representations, bringing them in this way closer to models" [MIT 10].

This decrease in complexity is also in part due to the ability of using digital environments to simulate a tridimensional vision, this without the need for 3D glasses, by simply continuously animating solids, as highlighted by Bakò [BAK 03]:

"Although the screens are two-dimensional and computers can produce only drawings, if we take time into account and use continuously changing pictures, it can help to giving the impression of a three dimensional vision".

However, even if digital representations allow us to surpass the limitations of planar projections, they remain planar representations and conserve the distance between representations and represented. This conservation of distance is, however, desirable, as it is essential for the student to transition successfully between drawings and sketches. Indeed, Laborde [LAB 99] considered that such programs "encourage the distinction between drawing and figure".

Bellemain [BEL 89] also suggests possibilities for these programs in terms of investigations using multiple possible tries and conjectures in situations of exploration or experimentation.

Finally, we note that even if studies on planar geometry programs have been carried out in primary or secondary schools, on the whole, studies on 3D geometry programs were carried out on high school students, leading us to question once more the possibility of these programs benefiting primary- or middle-school students. We shall therefore study the limits of these programs in order to try to understand the actual restrictions of their use.

### 1.4.2. *Limits of 3D geometry programs and consequences*

Even though they have advantages, 3D geometry programs are subject to certain limits. One of these is directly related to the HCI. Indeed, according to Chaachoua [CHA 97] who repeats elements already covered by Balacheff [BAL 94], the challenges of the interfaces of geometry programs in general, in particular of 3D geometry programs, are combined with didactic challenges (see Figure 1.21):

> "In all technological learning environment, the designers must make a choice as to the level of interface, and this through the internal universe. These choices can become specific constraints in the technological environment: both interface and content constraints. Objects of knowledge will therefore belong to a technological environment not only under the constraints of the didactic transposition but also under constraints specific to the technological environment, notion introduced by Balacheff [BAL 94a, p. 364]," [CHA 97].

Through the term internal universe, Balacheff implies all programming languages that may impact on the choices of interface implementation and development. In developing a geometry program, the choice of interfaces must not contradict those that should be made for didactic reasons.

Also, Chaachoua [CHA 97] advises what, alone, justifies this first chapter and illustrates by it the huge difficulty of HCI:

> "It is necessary to carry out *n* didactic analysis for the conception of a digital environment destine for teaching. For 3D geometry, this analysis has at least three poles: direct manipulation, representation choice and geometric primitives".

As highlighted by Mithalal [MIT 10], challenges are not limited to the interface of 3D geometrical programs but extend into that of the HCI. Indeed, to the potential navigational difficulties of menus is added the declaration difficulties of mathematical objects or even of the use of tools:

"It is important however to highlight that the use of these environments is in no part *natural*. Their complexity constrains the user – and more so the teacher – to learning the use of the program for themselves: declaration of objects, navigation of menus, use of tools.

Moreover, the representations produced by these programs have characteristics that need to be taken into account. This is particularly the case of resistance to movement properties of representations: they offer an increased experimentation field but assume a specific learning, as shown [RES 08]" [MIT 10].

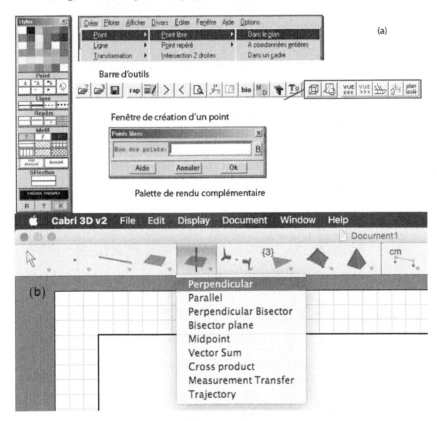

**Figure 1.21.** *Interfaces of the two most widely used programs: a) Geospace; b) Cabri-3D*

We may note that the digital 3D geometry environments require learning and that their use is not "natural". These points allow us to partially understand the fact that these programs are not advised during primary school. We can simply illustrate this by looking into the creation of one of the best known geometrical objects: the cube. For this, we will look at the interactions and manipulations necessary to create one using two 3D geometry programs. First is Geospace, the program candidates of the mathematics CAPES (a competitive teaching-qualification exam in France) have at their disposition, and the second is the current one, which is used as a reference by teachers due to its simplicity.

### 1.4.2.1. *Construction of a cube with Geospace*

In order to create a cube using Geospace, we must take the following steps:

1) Definition of a variable $a$ in order to modify the cube's dimensions using the following:

**[CREATE][NUMERICAL][REAL FREE VARIABLE]**

2) Choose a value for this variable:

**[NAVIGATE][CHOOSE FREE NUMERICAL VARIABLE]**

3) Place the 8 vertices in the reference using their coordinates: $A$ (0; 0; 0), $B$ ($a$; 0; 0), $C$ ($a$; $a$; 0), $D$ (0; $a$; 0), $E$ (0; 0; $a$), $F$ ($a$; 0; $a$), $G$ ($a$; $a$; $a$), $H$ (0; $a$; $a$)

**[CREATE][POINT REFERENCES][IN SPACE]**

4) Creation of the cube:

**[CREATE][SOLID][CONVEXE POLYHEDRON][DEFINED BY ITS VERTICES]**

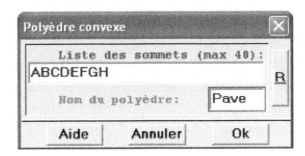

No fewer than 11 stages with 10 dialog boxes were necessary to create a cube with this program. Furthermore, we may note that regarding primary- and middle-school curricula, this would be beyond the capacity of their students, as 3D references are not covered at these stages until high school.

### 1.4.2.2. *Construction of a cube with Cabri-3D*

To create a cube using Cabri-3D, the process is as follows:

1) Select the tool "cube" in the regular polyhedron menu.

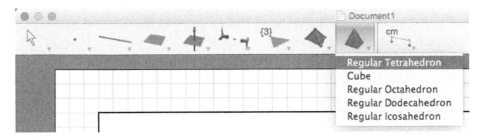

A contextual aide appears.

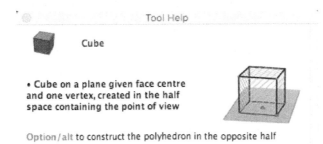

2) Choose the plane that contains one of the cube faces, then click to mark the center of this face.

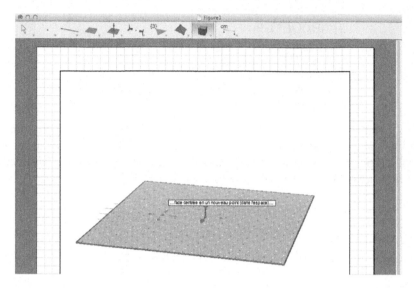

3) Position the cursor on the point corresponding to one of the vertices of the face, then click to create the cube.

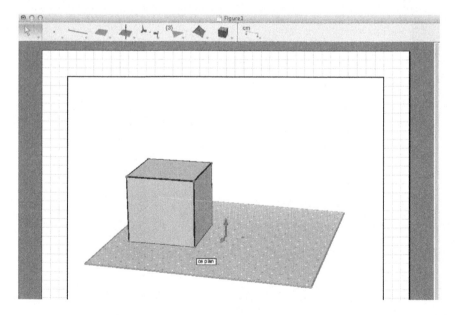

First note that nothing indicates which button corresponds to the regular polyhedrons in the tool menu (see Figure 1.22), its icon being very close to the one immediately to its left. Second, with Cabri-3D, 4 steps were necessary to create the cube.

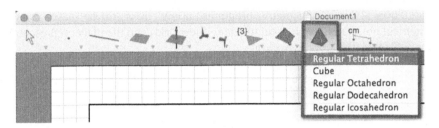

**Figure 1.22.** *Button on the tool bar allowing the choice of certain regular polyhedrons after clicking*

This brief presentation of the creation of a cube (which is supposed to be one of the most simple tasks) using two programs heavily used by teachers illustrates and confirms the theories of Restrepo [RES 08] and Mithalal [MIT 10], that is, the problems linked to interface and the need of a particular learning by children and teachers.

Balacheff [BAL 94] goes even further that the interface and interactions in terms of constraints. He mentions the "material constraints of digital supports" that are added to those of the interface. In 1994, Balacheff meant by "material constraints" those that were linked on the one hand to the operating system and programming language and on the other to the electronic components that make up the machines and that had a limited calculating ability. Nowadays, these technical constraints remain and even though the calculating ability has increased, questions are now arising about the mobility or the interactions between terminals. These additional "material constraints" lead us to question the relevance of desktops in the use of 3D geometry programs as well as on the possibility of using other technical means that may be better adapted. Indeed, we have seen that the use of these programs allows links to be made between the physical world and its planar representations. However, these are not continuous. Indeed, looking back at the example of Piaget's three mountains, it is possible to use a desktop to pivot the scene; however, it is physically impossible for the student to move the desktop and take the doll's position in order to check their answer.

### 1.4.3. *Partial conclusions and initial hypotheses*

In accordance with Chaachoua [CHA 97], we have carried out a theoretical didactic analysis on 3D geometry and its planar representation of everyday objects. First, this study lead us to the three following conclusions:

CONCLUSION 1.1.– 3D geometry programs allow links to be made between geometrical objects of the physical (the tangible world) and the planar representation of these objects (the graphic world).

CONCLUSION 1.2.– 3D geometry programs require specific learning and are not easily used by primary- and middle-school students.

CONCLUSION 1.3.– Classic materials, such as desktops, screens, keyboards and mouse, are not adapted to the use or implementation of 3D geometry programs.

From these three conclusions and our didactic analysis, we can already formulate the three following hypotheses:

HYPOTHESIS 1.1.– By using adapted technology and interactions, it is possible to render 3D geometry programs accessible to primary- and middle-school students.

HYPOTHESIS 1.2.– By using adapted technology and interactions, it is possible to create continuous links between physical objects from real life and their graphic planar representations.

It would therefore be possible to "create" a world in which both the real three-dimensional world as well as the two-dimensional graphical world would be situated, thus creating continuity in the passage between these two worlds. We can define this world as a 2D ½ world. Although this term already exists in video games and refers to graphic renditions, we shall here give it another meaning in the context of the transition between a tridimensional object and its planar representation.

DEFINITION 1.1.– *The 2D ½ world is defined in mathematics as the world that links real physical objects (tangible world) to the graphic world of planar representations of 3D objects. Here, objects are represented in 3D on two-dimensional supports and can be manipulated as in the tangible world without adding in particular constraints.*

We can now finally formulate one last hypothesis:

HYPOTHESIS 1.3.– By using adapted technology and interactions, it is possible to reduce students' cognitive charge such that they do not focus on the use of the 3D geometry program but on the concept being learnt, improving their learning.

Starting from these three hypotheses, we shall now study the technical choices offered and determine those that are most relevant in order to study the interactions to put into place in order to allow children aged 9 to 15 years to use a 3D geometry program. We will verify if under certain constraints it is possible to decrease the cognitive charge of students with the aim of focusing them not on the program, but on the learned concept.

2

# Mobile Devices and 3D Interactions

Nowadays, there are many different digital environments. Researchers and teachers have always been interested in the educational benefits that these different environments could have. It is also unsurprising to find studies and experiments with the arrival of each new technology in the public market. We can find nearly as many experimental fields as new materials that have presented a potential educational benefit. We can quote, for example, the first digital/multimedia rooms that are now present in nearly all school buildings (at least in middle schools). We can also remember the mobile classes that consisted of a trolley containing enough laptops for a classroom of children and with the facility to charge the laptops and provide Wi-Fi. Throughout history, there are experiments using technology for education: ultra-portable laptops that never managed to convince many; however, interactive blackboards (TBI) and virtual learning environment both became more commonplace. At present, many experiments are being carried out on tablets, and expectations are very high for this new technology (from the general public's point of view). According to the Éduscol website for the French National Education Ministry, no less than eight experiments are being carried out by the department of Corrèze where the Conseil Général has supplied all Year 7s with an iPad.

In the previous chapter, it was found that desktops are not necessarily the most suitable tools in the context of using a 3D geometry program. This hypothesis seems even more likely considering the fact that these programs are only available to high school students rather than those aged 9 to 15 years. Therefore, we may question the most suitable choice in terms of materials, followed by interactions to be put into place to allow students in the selected age range to be able to use the programs in such a way that they remain a tool in a learning process rather than a distraction to it.

In order to understand the choices that have been made throughout this study, we shall start by justifying the choice of mobile devices (MD) and more specifically tactile multi-touch tablets. Second, we shall present the different types of MDs as well as all the possible different entry systems. Next, we will briefly develop some points concerning mobile ergonomics before describing the state of the art of 3D interactive techniques on such devices. These interactive techniques mainly relate to the manipulation (translation, rotation and re-dimensioning) of 3D objects on MDs where the screen display is by nature two-dimensional. We will finish by presenting the languages and grammars of movements as well as a classification of the interactions.

## 2.1. Why mobile devices?

In our first educational chapter, we saw that dynamic geometry programs allowed students to create links between the real physical world of 3D objects and the graphical world of their planar representations. We have, however, also proven that these links are not continuous. Indeed, these programs are designed and destined for use on desktop computers or laptops. In any case, they are designed to be used on a static device by students. In this manner, the users are unable to change their position in order to observe the scene from different points of view, and instead are only able to rotate the scene. Even if the final result appears to be similar, this process corresponds neither to reality nor to what the user might wish to do in order to see the scene from another angle. In terms of teaching, these are two separate tasks in the development of 3D structure. To mitigate this problem, the first idea that comes to mind is to render the material mobile in order to allow the student to move. We could therefore imagine using a laptop for this, as 3D geometry programs are intended to work on this type of device. However, from this there is a second problem – how do we know the position of the laptop in relation to the screen as well as its orientation? Therefore, the addition of sensors to the laptop is a solution to this problem. In this context, it is interesting to consider current MD with already integrated sensors. Furthermore, these MDs have the advantage of generally being lighter, and therefore more easily handled in classrooms by students aged 9-15 years. There are three other main advantages to the use of a mobile terminal in our study. The first is the long tradition of using MDs in mathematics. The second is the potential educational benefit of this technology, shown by studies carried out, as we shall see, by the educational community in schools. Studies on MDs in education are not limited to the simple field, but also encompass the new relationships with knowledge they create as well as the continuity of school home work. Finally, the third advantage is based on the fact that MDs have been rapidly integrated into homes, which should mean the technology is accepted by its users.

### 2.1.1. *A long-standing tradition in mathematics*

Throughout the history of mathematics and its teaching, many different tools have been used, such as clay tablets, geometrical instruments (rulers, set-squares, compass, etc.), machines intended to facilitate calculations or more recently calculators and computers [MAS 10]. Since Roman times, efforts have been made to try and render these tools portable, for example, the abacus – a table (literally) for calculations and a version of which the Romans produced during the 1st Century (see Figure 2.1(a)). Similarly, the version that was commonly used (and still is) in Asia (see Figure 2.1(b)) is found in primary schools to help with numerical work (see Figure 2.1(c)).

(a)                    (b)                    (c)

**Figure 2.1.** *The first calculation tools in mathematics:*
*a) abacus (photograph by Mike Colshaw, CC BY SA 3.0, source: Wikipedia);*
*b) Chinese abacus; c) classroom abacus*

(a)                                      (b)

**Figure 2.2.** *a) A pascaline, signed by Pascal in 1652, found in the "arts et métiers"*
*museum in Paris (photograph by David Monniaux CC BY SA 3.0, source Wikipedia);*
*b) an educational version of the pascaline called "Zéro+1"*

Following these first calculation tools, the "pascaline" (see Figure 2.2(a)) was invented by Blaise Pascal [PAS 45] in 1642 in order to help his father (named superintendent of Haute-Normandie) who was tasked by Richelieu to reorder the perception of tax revenue. Nowadays, educational versions of the pascaline are still found in schools, under the name "Zéro+1" (see Figure 2.2(b)), with studies being carried out on its use in primary school [SOU 12]. From the 1960s, the use of calculators helped mitigate two main problems with computers of the time: their cost and size. First with four operations, followed by an increasing complexity in scientific, graphical and/or programmable calculators (see Figure 2.3), calculator use increased in schools and became the first MD to be commonly used in mathematics.

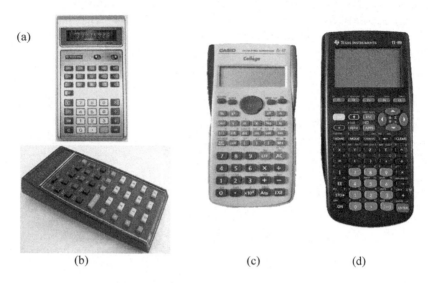

(a)

(b)              (c)              (d)

**Figure 2.3.** *Evolution of calculators from the ICC 804D made by Sanyo in 1971 to the TI-Nspire of nowadays: a) Sanyo, b) HP-35, c) Casio fx92, d) TI-89, shows that calculators, such as the TI-NSpire CX CAS, have truly become small laptops. (Teclasorg – Flickr. CC BY SA 2.0, source: Wikipedia)*

Although they have many different functions, they remain calculators rather than computers and the need for IT classrooms remains in place with their previously described limits. To these technical limits, we must add the organizational ones such as classroom bookings or even the need to plan hour-long sessions, even if they could be made shorter.

It is therefore easy to understand why MDs such as PC-tablets, tablets and even smartphones [SHI 11, ORF 13] are particularly attractive to a large number of both educational researchers and teachers. Indeed, the use of MDs can overcome the limitations linked to infrastructure as they can be used in standard classrooms, allowing the alternation of teaching moments requiring these devices with those where they are not needed [TRO 10]. There has been a noticeable development of a number of programs dedicated to teaching various subjects including mathematics.

Even if programs such as tracing-graphing programs in the use of functions (see Figure 2.4) are common, there are very few programs dedicated to 3D geometry and even fewer of them aimed at this type of investigation in primary–middle school.

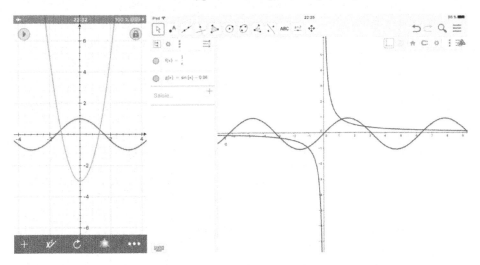

**Figure 2.4.** *Two iPhone programs of the "graphing-tracing" type for use in studying functions [TRO 10]. For a color version of this figure, see www.iste.co.uk/bertolo/geometry.zip*

Another important advantage of MDs is their popularity with students. Trouche and Drijvers [TRO 10] describe four reasons for this:

1) mobile terminals possess screens with a dynamic image display similar to television;

2) mobile terminals are familiar to students who use them confidently as they are permanently accessible;

3) students rapidly appropriate MTs due to the possibility of personalization, such as the installation of programs or personal games;

4) students feel free to try things and make mistakes.

Along with their popularity with students we can add the possibility of working in a network and the very attractive fact that, unlike with calculators, a mobile terminal can be used in transversal domains (homework, projects, etc.) as well as in subjects other than mathematics. The multitude of uses explains the interest of the educational community and we shall discuss its principles.

## 2.1.2. *Interest from the educational community*

In the literature review of the evaluation of the use of mobile and tactile e-learning and entertainment devices for young children, Michel *et al.* [MIC 11] highlight the benefits of using new mobile and tactile technology:

"One of the challenges in researching the domain of learning in young children (3-10 years old) is to take advantage of new mobile and tactile technology. Indeed, thanks to ubiquitous technology, learning can become less formal and take place in different contexts (locations, access to resources, interactions with other learners or tutors, etc.) and at any time. This ensures the continuity of learning practices between school and the outside world (home or other locations) by giving access to a group of learning and entertaining activities (broadcasted by downloads, live access, videos on demand, etc.) as well as personalized learning pathways. The work carried out outside school can therefore be considered as an integral part of the learning experience without breaking from schoolwork".

Despite this study being based on the 3–10 years age range, it remains true for students of any age. Mobile devices, through their ubiquity, create continuity between school and home. The study by Kerawalla *et al.* [KER 07] shows significantly positive results in numerical learning for students using tablet-PCs to do their homework, a school–home continuity.

Martin and Ertzberger [MAR 13] show in their study that the use of MDs in a type of teaching they call "here and now learning", is not the miracle solution to the various problems of teaching. The study shows benefits to investing in this type of learning but students' results remain better with the use of classical desktops rather than with the use of MDs. Several studies [FAL 13, KUC 14] show the importance of design, content and functionalities for MD programs aimed at the education sector.

In a recent Canadian study by Karsenti and Fievez [KAR 13], 16 main advantages from scientific literature were put forward for the use of MDs and particularly tablets:

"Within the main advantages of the use of tactile tablets in a scholarly context, it is found that for students:

1) motivation is increased (see [KIN 12, SAC 12, WAI 12]);

2) accessing, editing and sharing information is facilitated (see [BAB 13, FRI 12, HAH 112, MAR 13]);

3) learning and performances of students is eased (see [CHU 12, FER 13, ISA 12, LAU 12, MCK 12, OST 13, ROS 12]);

4) learning strategies are more varied (see [FER 13]);

5) individualized learning is increased (see [MCC 12, WAS 13]);

6) reading experience is improved (see [FER 13, HUB 12, SLO 12, ZAM 112]);

7) communication and collaboration are increased, both between the students themselves and between the students and the teacher (see [GEI 11,  HEN 12, HUT 12]);

8) technologic competencies are improved [HUB 12, KIL 12];

9) student creativity is higher [SUL 13];

10) the portability and mobility of the device are extended (see [HEN 12, HIL 12, KIN 13, VIL 12, WIL 11]);

11) evaluation of students is facilitated [ALB 12, ISA 12];

12) quality of educational supports is improved [MUR 11];

13) learning to write is facilitated [MUR 11];

14) the organization of work is more efficient [CHU 12];

15) the presentation of school work by students is improved [MUR 11];

16) the advantages for students with learning difficulties are high [MCC 12]".

Even if the previous studies are centered on the advantages of MDs for students, it is interesting to note that studies are also being carried out on how teachers are accepting this technology, with more mixed points of view [IFE 13]. According to Ifenthaler and Schweinbenz [IFE 13], the involvement of teachers with this type of technology is linked to their conception of teaching. So, teachers who place the students at the center of the educational facility are more receptive to the use of new technology in their classroom. Furthermore, in their conclusion, Karsenti and Fievez [KAR 13] highlight a major disadvantage to the use of tablets such as iPads: student distraction.

> "The collected data has allowed us to identify many challenges met by both students and teachers, both during questioning but also during the many group interviews carried out. We shall set out the nine main ones:
>
> 1) the first challenge met by teachers, seemingly a major one, is that of the student *distraction* caused by tactile tablets. They allow students, perhaps too easily, to not listen to the teacher. And, young as they are, students have discovered electronic messaging and social media, which, very often, will distract their attention [...];
>
> 2) finally, several students and teachers have suggested that the use of tablets, possibly because of the distraction, could harm their academic success" [KAR 13].

If there is a lot of interest from the educational community in MDs, it is in part related to the fact that there is still some reality in the field of penetration of this technology, whether in homes or schools.

### 2.1.3. *A field reality*

We have seen that many experiments with MDs have been carried out in France. This is obviously the case in many other countries. In the introduction of their paper, Karsenti and Fievez [KAR 13] suggest that more than 10,000 students use a tablet on a daily basis in class. In the United States, this number is already more than 4.5 million [ETH 13]. In New Zealand, certain schools insist that parents equip their children with the following:

> "Some schools have even gone as far as insisting parents procure for their child such a device, in much the same way as purchasing books on a stationery list" [IHA 13].

During some of our experiments in our program, we asked students from two classes, one of Year 6 (29 students) and another of Year 7 (21 students), whether they already owned a tactile MD such as a tablet or smartphone or whether they had already used one at least once before the beginning of this experiment. It appeared that:

– 98% of the students surveyed had already used a tablet or smartphone;

– 94% of students owned at least one of these devices at home and 56% at least two;

– 68% of students owned their own tablet or smartphone;

– in cases where there is only one device in a household, 32% of the time it belongs to the child.

We also asked about different uses of these two types of device. Figure 2.5 summarizes these results. We may note that even if the main use is entertainment, work comes in fourth with 32% of use, thus appearing non-negligible.

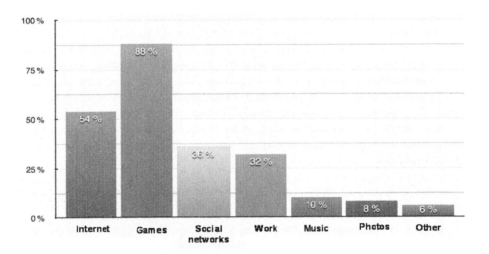

**Figure 2.5.** *Different uses of tablets and smartphones of 50 Year 6-7 students in 2014*

We have seen the different uses of MDs. However, several different types exist with different particularities, each with their own advantages and disadvantages. We shall now study the different MDs, which will lead us to our choice of material for our own experiments.

## 2.2. Mobile devices

As we have previously seen, several types of MDs exist and a large number of these have been used in an educational context, at least experimentally. In this section, we shall first define exactly what is meant by MD or at least what we limit ourselves to in an educational context, and then we will list the different devices that correspond to it. Second, we will study the different entrance and exit systems of these MDs in order to encompass those that may be useful to the set up of interactions in the context of learning dynamic geometry. Finally, we shall explicitly state our technical choice for one of these MDs.

### 2.2.1. *Different types of mobile devices*

The term mobile device encompasses a large number of portable units that treat and exchange data in mobile situations. The first MDs were mobile data terminals (MDT) and were found in professional cars such as police cars, taxis and ambulances. These devices, most often functioning using radiowaves, allowed the communication with a central and the exchange of information through a screen and often a keyboard.

In this context, linked to the learning of 3D geometry, it seems irrelevant to spend time on MDs linked to vehicles, and so we shall simply review the most used MDs for the development of educational or educational and entertainment programs. In this way, we can restrict ourselves to MDs such as smartphones, tablets, game consoles and ultra-portable laptops. We set aside classical laptops, these being more often used as desktops and of such a weight that a child could not realistically use in a mobile situation.

In this chapter, we shall consider that MDs adapted to teaching have the following characteristics:

– a group of components assembled into a single device, unlike a classic desktop, and therefore without the need to use a keyboard, mouse or even a screen;

– weight and size that allow it to be used in situations of mobility, which, in our context, will allow the student to move about easily within the classroom;

– a large autonomy that will allow its use in class without interruption during student activities;

– an autonomous functioning that allows a mobile class-style use, with the possibility of quick and practical transport between classes;

– the possibility of connecting to a network (Wi-Fi, Bluetooth, 3G or 4G) that will allow the connection to either an external network, such as the Internet via Wi-Fi, or an ad hoc network created within the classroom;

– the possibility of installing educational or entertainment-based programs.

We shall now briefly describe the five types of device that correspond to the six characteristics of MDs just stated.

### 2.2.1.1. *Mobile phones/smartphones*

Mobile phones appeared approximately 30 years ago. In 1983, Motorola commercialized the first of these, called the Motorola DynaTAC 8000X. This 800 g phone measured 25 cm (not including the antenna) had the freedom of one hour's worth of telephone calls and naturally could only be used for calling. Over the next 24 years, mobile phones continued to evolve. First, from the hardware point of view, thus reducing their weight and size while increasing battery capacity as well as self-sufficiency. Second, the software evolved through the addition of more and more functionalities such as calendars, alarm clocks and the ability to take pictures, followed by the Internet connection, until they slowly became smartphones. In 2007 with the arrival Apple's iPhone, this evolution took a new turn by making devices with the capacity of small computers equipped with a multipoint touchscreen available to the general public, the functioning of which we shall study later. The ability to install programs on these new smartphones has once again increased the field of use of these phones, of which telephone calls are not necessarily the primary function.

### 2.2.1.2. *Portable video game consoles*

The first portable video game console dates from 1979 and was called Milton Bradley's Microvision. The Nintendo Game Boy that popularized this type of console followed it in 1989. Currently, the two largest players in this market are Nintendo with the 3DS (or 2DS) and Sony with the Portable PlayStation (PSP). Although uncommon for both types of console, educational games do exist and some developers have tried to develop specific educational programs for them.

The main characteristic of these consoles is that they have the ability to render good 3D images. Nintendo consoles are even equipped with touchscreens.

We may also note that for many years, a great deal of research has been carried out on teaching and/or education as well as on video games [AGU 03, DON 07].

### 2.2.1.3. *Ultra mobile*

Ultra-mobile computers are simply another version of classic laptops. They share the same operating system and are simply smaller, with screen diagonals of 10-12 inches. They became popular due to their portability but are currently overtaken in the market by tablets, which possess the same size screens but with greater autonomy and higher versatility due to the large number of programs that are either free or low cost.

We shall note that these ultra-mobile laptops can be separated into two categories: ultra-mobile PCs and tablet PCs. The first are reduced-size mobile computers, whereas the latter are mobile PCs equipped with a touchscreen and often with a stylus that allows interactions with the screen. These are where current tactile tablets originate.

### 2.2.1.4. *Tablets*

The first "wide audience" tablet was developed by the Grid Systems Corporation and produced by Samsung in 1989 and was known as GRIDPad. It used the MS-DOS operating system, had a 640 × 400 pixel screen with a stylus and cost a modest 3000 \$ (or 2790 € at the exchange rate of the time, with an average salary in France being 1224 € per month). In 1993, various companies such Amstrad with the Pen Pad Amstrad (1993) or even Apple with the Newton MessagePad (see Figure 2.6(a)) developed personal assistants with touchscreens. These MDs did not meet a roaring commercial success. In 2001, Microsoft launched the tablet-PC (see Figure 2.6(b)), which was a computer equipped with the Windows XP operating system, modified to take into account the use of the touchscreen with a stylus as well as the recognition of handwriting. It was not until 2007 with the launch of the iPhone that Apple developed another touchscreen tablet, launched in 2010: the iPad (see Figure 2.6(c)). From its first version, the iPad was integrated with a multipoint screen, capable of simultaneously treating 11 points of contact as well as an accelerometer. One year later, Samsung commercialized the Galaxy Tab. These new generations of tablets function with the same operating systems as smartphones and generally have the same technical characteristics with one difference: the larger screen size of tablets. With many programs to download, they are easily configured and even personalized. Being greatly less expensive than touchscreen boards and with a greater self-sufficiency than laptops and ultra-mobile laptops, they were quickly tested by many schools.

Currently, tablets are equipped with multipoint touchscreens (generally with a diagonal length of 11 inches), an accelerometer, a gyroscope, a camera and are capable of connecting to a Wi-Fi, Bluetooth, 3G or 4G network. Easily able to reach self-sufficiencies of 10 hours, they are easily configured and even reach the same performances as many laptops. All these characteristics make them very attractive polyvalent devices.

a)                                      b)                                      c)

**Figure 2.6.** *Evolution of touchscreen tablets between 1989 and nowadays: a) Newton MessagePad (photograph by Rama, CC BY SA 2.0, source: Wikipedia); b) Lenovo Yoga 3 (photograph by Maurizio Pesce, CC BY 2.0, source: Wikipedia); c) iPad Air*

**Figure 2.7.** *Different types of mobile devices*[1]

## 2.2.2. *Entry systems of mobile terminals*

From their characteristics to their compactness, MDs use entry systems that are either adapted or different from those that may be found on classic desktops. We shall briefly describe these systems.

### 2.2.2.1. *Keyboard / Buttons*

If all these tactile or otherwise MDs have one thing in common, it is the presence of at least one mechanical button (at least the on–off button). A large number of mobile phones and ultra-mobile laptops have a numerical keypad and/or a keyboard made up of mechanical buttons (see Figure 2.8(a)). Most tablets are equipped with a

---

1 Photographs by Evan Amos, Rafael Fernandez, Cserlajos, Rev8600, Redrum0486 (CC BY SA 3.0); Red (CC BY 3.0); Android Open Source Project (CC BY 2.5); Sinchen Lin (CC BY 2.0). Source: Wikipedia.

tactile software keyboard (see Figure 2.8(b)) that appears on the screen on demand and that can be adapted to suit different needs. During the implementation of the program, several keyboard configurations are suggested and are usually customizable (see Figure 2.8(c)). The main disadvantage of these keyboards is that they obscure a large part of the screen, leaving little space for the visualization of data. In the case of mechanical keyboards, they have the same advantages and disadvantages as desktop keyboards with the added disadvantage of the size of the keys generally being reduced.

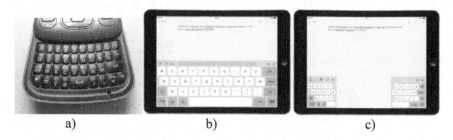

a)                          b)                                    c)

**Figure 2.8.** *Different MD keyboards: a) a BlackBerry's mechanical keyboard; b) keyboard program of the iPad; c) separated keyboard in the iPad*

## 2.2.2.2. Joysticks

Whether they are physical or programmable, joysticks are present in many MDs. Initially an integral part of video games, they are found in some mobile phones (see Figures 2.9(a)) as well as in ultra-mobile laptops, and even when this is not the case, the presence of Bluetooth allows them to connect to one. Tablets are able to have programs installed and among these are many games. Initially, these games made use of virtual joysticks (see Figure 2.9(b)) to allow gamers to recreate the previous user experience. There are now several examples of physical joysticks, adapted to tablets (see Figure 2.9(c)).

a)                              b)                                c)

**Figure 2.9.** *Different types of joysticks on mobile phones and tablets: a) joystick on a mobile phone; b) virtual joystick; c) physical and adaptable joystick for tablet or smartphone*

## 2.2.2.3. *Touchscreens*

### 2.2.2.3.1. A bit of history

Contrary to popular belief, the first tactile system was not invented by developers but by a composer, Hugh Le Caine, the creator of electronic music. Between 1945 and 1948, he developed a prototype named "saqueboute", the ancestor of synthesizers. The musician could play with his or her right hand and control its tone with the left, each finger being able act on a distinct command by taking into account the pressure applied (see Figure 2.10(a)). The index finger was used to move a device aimed at modifying the shape of the waves via a mobile pad (see Figure 2.10(b)).

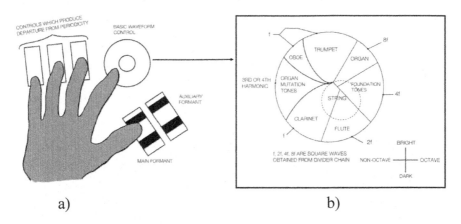

a)                                                              b)

**Figure 2.10.** *First tactile system, the saqueboute from 1948: a) left hand commands; b) device controlled by the index finger with the pad represented by the dotted line*

It was not until 1972 that the first touchscreen was commercialized. It equipped the PLATO IV (programmed logic for automatic teaching operations) that was designed and developed by researchers from the University of Illinois. This screen was mono-point, that is, it only detected a single point of contact and was not sensitive to pressure. Interestingly, it was also the first plasma screen.

In 1981, Jack Rebman created the first system of sensors able to recognize several points of contact [WOL 81]. This device was able to detect shapes and their orientation. One year later, in 1982, Nimish Mehta [MEH 82] from the University of Toronto designed the first multi-point surface for HCI. It was made up of a matte glass panel with optical properties, allowing it to have a white background with black contact points when a finger touched the panel. A camera located behind the panel collected images that were then processed. The Mehta device could not only recognize contact points but also shapes.

In 1984, Boie *et al.* created the first multi-touch screen using a capacitating device that covered a cathode ray tube (CRT) screen. In 1985, Lee *et al.* designed a multi-touch tablet able to recognize the position and pressure applied on each contact point. In 1986, Buxton and Myers invented the first bi-manual system in which one hand controlled the arrangement while the other controlled the scaling, these being simultaneous and independent operations. All these systems had one point in common that they were all made up of two distinct layers. The first was to receive the tactile elements, while the second displayed the result.

In 1991, Bill Buxton and Brad A Myers introduced two-directional technology that consisted of one element for both the entrance and exit. In 2001, Paul Dietz and Darren Leigh [DIE 01] from the Mitsubishi laboratory in Cambridge launched the DiamondTouch (see Figure 2.11(a)) capable of distinguishing between fingers and hands as well as complex movements. This tactile tablet also allowed users to work collaboratively. In 2005, Jefferson Han [HAN 05] launched a new multipoint system that was easily fabricated and at lower cost. Finally in 2007, Microsoft launched the tactile Surface table and Apple the iPhone, thus popularizing tactile surfaces (see Figures 2.11(b) and (c)).

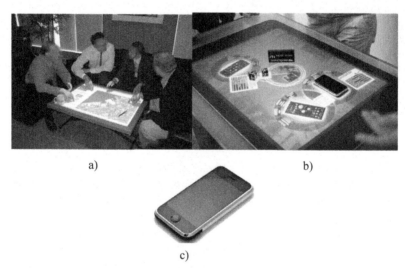

a)                                          b)

c)

**Figure 2.11.** *Different tactile systems since 1991: a) DiamondTouch (photograph by MERL, CC BY SA 3.0, source: Wikipedia); b) Microsoft Surface (photograph by Ergonomidesign, CC BY SA 3.0, source: Wikipedia); c) Apple iPhone*

Currently, tactile devices require five different main technologies that we shall now briefly describe.

## 2.2.2.3.2. Capacitive

This is the oldest of tactile technologies. A metallic and conductive surface is added to the screen. Next, from the four corners of the screen, tension is applied to this layer, thus creating a uniform magnetic field. When the user touches the screen, it becomes a part of the electrical circuit and a small part of the current is taken off at the point of contact (see Figure 2.12). The value of the current is measured in the four corners and is proportional to the distance of the point of contact. The calculation of the ratio of the different values accurately gives the coordinates of the contact point.

We shall note that the contact must take place with a conductive material, thus explaining, for example, the development of gloves possessing conductive parts on the tips of the fingers to allow the use of smartphones or tablets in winter.

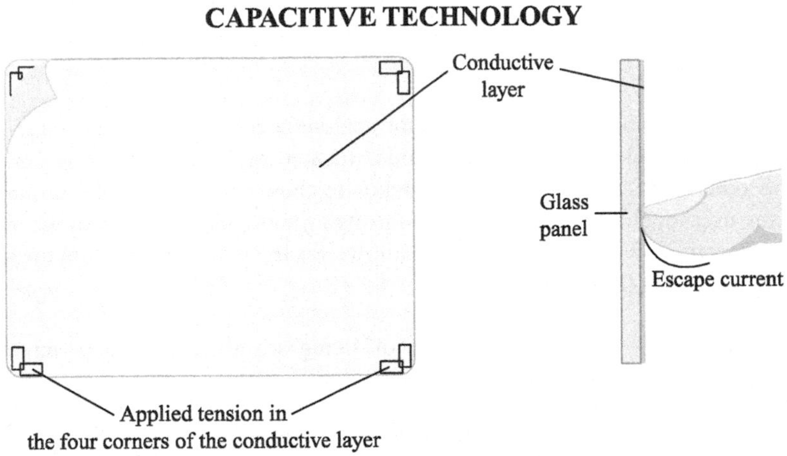

### CAPACITIVE TECHNOLOGY

**Figure 2.12.** *Description of capacitive technology [MES 01]*

## 2.2.2.3.3. Resistive

This technology is mainly used in industry, as it is very robust. Resistive technology consists of assembling two conductive layers separated by an isolating layer. When the user touches the screen, the two conductive layers come into contact locally, thus modifying the current distribution across the surface. Measuring the tensions allows for the calculation of the position of the point of contact (see Figure 2.13).

Unlike capacitive technology, resistive technology is more resistant to scratches and can be used with normal gloves.

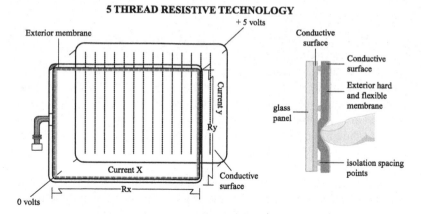

**Figure 2.13.** *Description of resistive technology [MES 01]*

### 2.2.2.3.4. Infrared

Infrared technology is based on a light grid situated in front of the screen. This grid is created by electroluminescent diodes located on two boards, one horizontal and the other vertical to the screen. Opposite these diodes are phototransistors. When the user touches the screen, it cuts through the infrared beams and the absence of light detection on the phototransistors allows for the calculation of the position of the point of contact (see Figure 2.14).

This technology has the advantage of being installed over any screen, but remains expensive and is relatively low in accuracy.

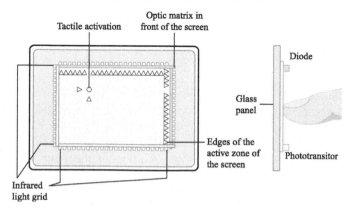

**Figure 2.14.** *Description of infrared technology [MES 01]*

## 2.2.2.3.5. Surface waves

This is the most recent of all interface tactile technologies. It is based on piezoelectric transducers placed to one horizontal and one vertical side of the screen, which transform an electrical signal into ultrasonic waves. These waves are propagated along a glass slab that is superimposed with the screen (see Figure 2.15). Opposite these emitting transducers are placed receiving ones. When the user touches the screen, it absorbs part of the wave, modifying its arrival time at the receiving transducer. As the speed of wave propagation and the size of the screen are both known, we are able to precisely calculate the point of contact.

This technology also allows us to measure the quantity of energy absorbed in order to obtain information regarding depth component.

**SURFACE WAVE TECHNOLOGY**

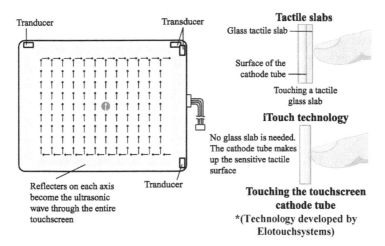

**Figure 2.15.** *Description of surface wave technology [MES 01]*

## 2.2.2.3.6. FTIR (frustrated total internal reflection)

Frustrated total internal reflection (FTIR) technology was developed by Han in 2005 [HAN 05]. It is based on one or more infrared cameras placed behind a semi-transparent surface. Infrared radiation is emitted onto a reflective surface. When the user touches the screen, the propagation of infrared light is deviated. The cameras sense this deviation and an image treatment algorithm determines the point of contact.

This technology allows the determination of both size and shape of contact. It has been used in several commercial products such as the Microsoft Surface table or the Immersion CubeTile [RIV 08]. Its main disadvantages are the latent time linked to video treatment and the cumbersome system requiring a certain amount of space.

### 2.2.2.4. Sensors

Last generation mobile phones and tablets are massively equipped with all types of sensors. Some of the main ones are:

– global positioning system (GPS), allowing us to know geographical coordinates;

– electronic compass that shows the orientation of the MD;

– accelerometer measuring the acceleration;

– gyroscope that measures the angular speed of movement.

All of these sensors allow for the exploration of new interactions using MD. From 2000, Hinckley *et al.* [HIN 00] used sensors to determine the orientation of the MD or to scroll through the pages. These interactions are now possible on all MDs. In 2010, Ketabdar *et al.* suggested a system based on magnetic sensors [KET 10]. The user, equipped with a magnetic ring, is able to interact with the MD through movements around it, with the advantage, compared with a camera, of not having occultation problems.

### 2.2.2.5. Camera

The progress of the last few years, both in terms of the improvement of the optical sensors as well as the treatment of numerical images, has meant that the vast majority of MDs are equipped with cameras. Not only are these able to be used instead of digital cameras, but also they are able to film in High Definition (HD). Many MDs also now have two cameras, making it possible during video-conferences to show what is being seen without having to stop looking at the camera. The appearance of cameras in MDs has also meant that new innovative interactions have been explored. In 2005, Hachet, Pouderoux and Guitton explored the possibility of an interface based on a camera and able to interact with a MD [HAC 05a]. In 2011, the i3D program that uses the user's point of view to interact with 3D scenes on an MD [FRA 11] created ripples through the community and was downloaded one million times in 3 days.

### 2.2.2.6. Microphone

The majority of MDs are equipped with microphones. From the beginning it was obvious that a mobile phone needs a microphone in order to communicate; the development of communications such as "Voice over IP" (VoIP) made the presence of microphones almost unavoidable on MDs with an Internet connection. The presence of these microphones also allows the use of vocal commands on MDs.

Nevertheless, in an educational context, this entry system is not advised as one can easily imagine the difficulty of managing a class of 30 students, each talking to use the vocal commands.

### 2.2.2.7. Our choice

We have chosen to develop our program and carry out studies on a multi-touch tactile tablet such as Apple's iPad (see Figure 2.16).

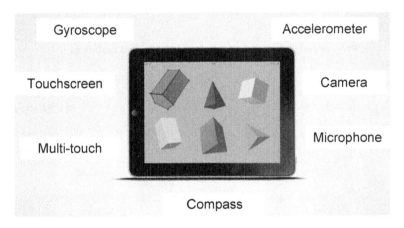

**Figure 2.16.** *Our choice: iPad tablets due to their interactive possibilities*

Our choice was made for three main reasons:

1) At the beginning of this study, this tablet offered the most interactive possibilities due to its equipment (see Figure 2.16):

i) a tactile and multi-touch screen able to process 11 points of contact;

ii) two cameras : one on each side;

iii) a microphone;

iv) an accelerometer;

v) a gyroscope : at the time of our choice, only the iPad had this kind of sensor.

Following this, two more possibilities were added to the iPad:

i) a digital compass;

ii) a GPS.

2) As the iPad was the first tablet on the market, the first experiments were carried out on them and they were also the first to be introduced into schools. At the start of our study, the iPad was nearly the only tablet present in schools.

3) From the start, the popularity of tablets, particularly the iPad but followed by the Samsung Galaxy Tab was high. This popularity leads us to believe that the penetration potential of these tablets into homes and schools was high. This was confirmed, as is shown by the evolution of the sales of digital materials (see Figure 2.17).

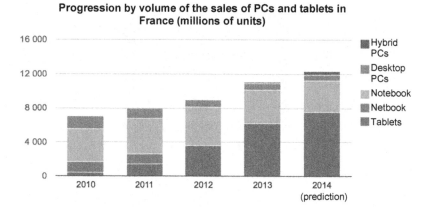

**Figure 2.17**. *Evolution of PC and tablet sales in France between 2010 and 2014 (Source GFK - via ZDNet.fr/chiffres-cles). For a color version of this figure, see www.iste.co.uk/bertolo/geometry.zip*

## 2.3. Interactions on mobile devices and physiology

Interactions on MDs are limited by different ergonomic and usability constraints to desktops. Their mobile character obviously allows the user to move around with the device and often will continue to interact with it during these movements. In the case of use in a classroom and a learning context encompassing the end of primary to middle school, these constraints must be taken into account. Indeed, students can move around to work in groups or to present their results to the class using a projector and their tablet.

### 2.3.1. *Specificities of mobile devices*

The first specificity of MDs obviously resides in their ubiquitous use. Although Karlson *et al.* [KAR 07] showed that users prefer MDs such as smartphones with one hand only, for tablets used in a mobile situation, the preference is for two: one to hold the tablet and the other to interact with it. We were able to note that when children use tablets while on the move or standing to demonstrate something, the tablet is often set on the forearm of the non-dominant arm with interactions taking place using the dominant arm. However, even if movement is possible and even desirable, most of the time the tablet is used stationary on the student's desk, whether for individual or group work. In the latter case, the student will rotate the screen to show the group. It seems important to concentrate on uni-manual interactions for simple and common movements that will be carried out by moving around or by holding the tablet.

The second specificity of MDs resides in their reduced size, and therefore a restricted surface use of the screen. Based on the work of Chittaro [CHI 06] on the visualization of information on MDs as well as the work of Brewster [BRE 02] that suggests using multi-modality to decrease menu size, Decle, in his PhD thesis insists on the importance of "not overloading the display, particularly by limiting the use of *menus*, which occupy a large proportion of the screen" [DEC 09]. This suggestion, added to the fact that in the context of 3D geometry programs there is an additional interface problem, leads us to investigate possibilities such as interfaces with no menus in the classic meaning of the word.

To the problem of screen size is added, for a certain number of MDs, the problem of touchscreen visualization. In the case of tablets and particularly iPads, which we have chosen as our material support in these experiments, the screen is tactile and multi-touch. This characteristic allows the use of one or more fingers (or a stylus) in interactions with the screen. However, a study by Vogel *et al.* [VOG 09] showed that in the use of a 12-inch tablet-PC, the arm covers 47% of the screen. Several studies have found solutions to this problem, by using either a transparent screen or two screens (on in front of and the other behind the device). In 2006 and 2007, Wigdor *et al.* [WIG 06, WIG 07] first suggested a table, followed by a tablet named the "LucidTouch", with a double touchscreen. In 2009, Shen *et al.* [SHE 09] suggested a multi-touch double-face MD. Based on these works, Sauret *et al.* [SAU 11] in 2011 suggested a slide and drop interaction on this kind of device.

Constraints linked to tablets are added to those linked to human psychology.

### 2.3.2. *Limitations due to physiologic characteristics*

#### 2.3.2.1. *Imprecision of fingers*

As we have just seen, the issue with screen covering is important when it comes to the use of MDs with touchscreens. Not only is there a problem when it comes to covering the screen with the forearm, but also that of covering part of the screen with the finger at its point of contact. Indeed, it seems obvious that a finger (even that of a child) is larger than a mouse's cursor. Holz and Baudisch, through two studies [HOL 10, HOL 11] showed the lack of precision of a finger during a target choosing task.

Alongside techniques using a double-surface device, many techniques on current devices have been suggested to mitigate this lack of precision, for example, Shift [VOG 07], which consists of making the zone covered by the finger appear zoomed and shifted, then adding a cursor to select the desired point (see Figure 2.18(a)). Selection is carried out once the finger is lifted. Apple used this solution in its touchscreen devices. TapTap and MagStick are also examples of this [ROU 08]. TapTap consisted in double taps, the first zoomed the zone around the point of contact and the second tap selected the target (see Figure 2.18(b)). MagStick created a shifted cursor from the initial point of contact. By moving the finger, a telescopic stick appears with an opposite direction to that of the finger.

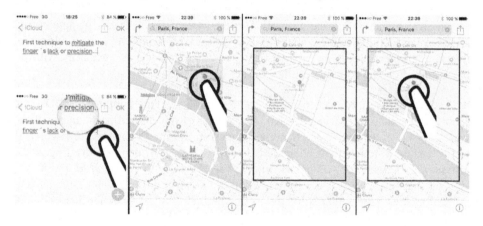

**Figure 2.18.** *Two techniques to mitigate the finger's lack of precision: a) Shift; b) TapTap*

### 2.3.2.2. *Characteristics of the hand*

The problems linked to the use of fingers have just been described. Touchscreen tablets are however composed of multi-touch screens that allow the use of several fingers at once, recognized as several points of contact. The study by Wand *et al.* [WAN 09] shows the use of the detection of the shape of the contact zone of one or more fingers, its size and orientation in selection and designation tasks. However, this study also shows that in the case of several-finger use, they should not belong to the same hand, limiting the use of this information to two fingers. Indeed, from the moment two fingers from the same hand are considered, any movement from one can cause a parasitic movement in the other, despite the 23 degrees of freedom in a hand [AND 92]. It is therefore important to take into account the physiological particularities in the set up of multi-touch gestures, this even more so considering that children's motor skills are evolving in our studied age range.

When we justified our choice of tablet, we put forward the large number of possible interactions due to the various components such as the integrated sensors. Many motor racing games make use of the accelerometer to steer the vehicle by holding the tablet as if it were a steering wheel (see Figure 2.19). Even if the use of sensors can introduce additional interactions to those already linked to touchscreens, certain physiological limitations must be taken into account. The study by Rahman [RAH 09] shows that the hand is able to move up to 60° in flexion and 45° in extension (see Figure 2.20(a)), up to 65° in pronation and 60° in supination (see Figure 2.20(b)) and finally, up to 15° in ulnar deviation and 30° in radial deviation (see Figure 2.20 (c)). These limitations must be taken into account in the development of interactions using sensors.

**Figure 2.19.** *Asphalt 6 on iPhone using the accelerometer to steer the car [DEC 09]*

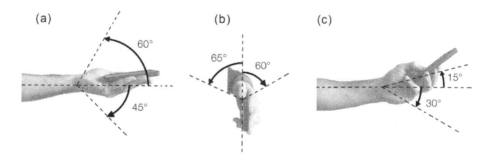

**Figure 2.20.** *Illustration of the limits to hand movement, application limits: a) in flexion/extension; b) pronation/supination; c) ulnar/radial deviations [RAH 09]*

## 2.4. 3D interaction techniques

In this section, we shall study the different types of interactions allowing a user to interact with the 3D environment. Despite technological advances and research already carried out into 3D interactions, these remain a challenge. Indeed, the difficulty is in manipulating an object in three dimensions with, most of the time, an entry and exit system in two dimensions (mouse, touchscreen, etc.). In their 2001 study, Bowman *et al.* [BOW 01] grouped 3D interactions into three categories: navigation, selection/manipulation and system control.

So, after some brief mathematical reminders, we shall suggest a group of 3D interactions, taking into account the different possibilities allowed by an iPad-style tablet (touchscreen, sensors and camera) for two out of three of Bowman's categories. We will not cover the system control interactions as they do not fall under our working remit.

### 2.4.1. *Mathematical reminders*

Before covering the state of the art in 3D interactions, it is important to come back to a few mathematical points that will be useful throughout the whole of the book and, in particular, during the description of the interactions we developed and/or evaluated.

#### 2.4.1.1. *References*

In 3D geometry, whatever the task: navigation or selection/manipulation, the task is relative to a given reference. Three-dimensional programs, however, generally use different references depending on the action to be carried out. There are four main Cartesian references (see Figure 2.21), generally orthonormal:

– the *world reference*: the reference that defines the 3D environment and its origin. Two of its axes are used to define the plane representing the ground and the third is orthogonal to it;

– the *camera reference* or *observer's reference*: here, the main point of view is considered to be the origin and generally the Z-axis defines the orientation of sight;

– the *screen reference*: two of the axes are parallel to the edge of the screen and the third is orthogonal to the plane of the screen. This reference is used to determine the position of a pixel on the screen as well as its depth using the ZBuffer (depth stamp);

– the *object's reference* or *model reference*: each object of the scene has its own reference that is centered on the object itself and where the origin is generally located at the object's center of gravity. The axes depend on the orientation of the object in space.

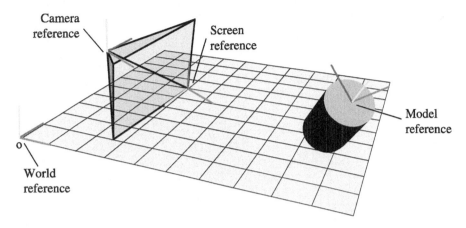

**Figure 2.21.** *Different references used in 3D programs (source image, [DEC 09])*

### 2.4.1.2. *Transformations*

The manipulation of various objects in space are nearly all carried out using three mathematical transformations, which are: translation, rotation and homothety. There are obviously other types of mathematical transformations such as screwing but this is simply made up of a rotation followed by a translation for which the direction is parallel to the axis of rotation.

### 2.4.1.2.1. Translations

Translations are without a doubt the simplest of planar or 3D transformations. They are linked to the notion of vectors, which allow them to give the direction and length of the translation (see Figure 2.23(a)). This transformation depends, as do the following, on the reference in which they are defined.

### 2.4.1.2.2. Rotations

Three-dimensional rotations are always defined by a rotation axis and an angle. In other words, in mathematics, rotations about a point in space do not exist (see Figure 2.23(b)). Rotations are isometries and so conserve lengths and angles. Rotations are also movements in space and so conserve orientation as well. In the case of transformations in 3D digital scenes, matrices of rotations are often used.

In order to define the orientation of an object, different from its rotation, Euler's angles (see Figure 2.22) or quaternions are used. The use of quaternions gives a more practical mathematical language to represent the orientation and rotation of a 3D object.

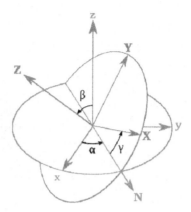

**Figure 2.22.** *Euler's angles: the xyz system (fixed) is shown in blue, the XYZ system (rotation) in red. The knotted line, marked N, appears in green (source Wikipedia). For a color version of this figure, see www.iste.co.uk/bertolo/geometry.zip*

### 2.4.1.2.3. Homotheties

Homotheties are transformations that are defined by an invariant point and a real value, k called ratio, giving the point M' that is the image of M by $\overrightarrow{OM'} = k\overrightarrow{OM}$. More simply, homotheties are enlargements/reductions (see Figure 2.23 (c)). From a digital and practical point of view, these homotheties can be carried out using either one or two axes.

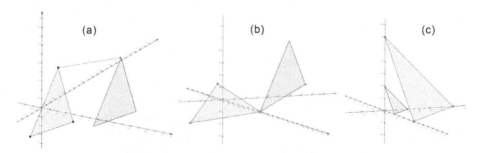

**Figure 2.23.** *Illustration of different mathematical 3D transformations: a) translation, b) rotation; c) homothety*

## 2.4.1.2.4. Degrees of freedom

After a quick reminder of several mathematical elements that will be used throughout the book and that will help with the general understanding, we must now define the concept of degrees of freedom, the link with the three transformations presented above. Initially a concept based in medicine (the hand has 23 degrees of freedom) and mechanics, a degree of freedom (DOF) is the possibility for an object to carry out a transformation (translation or rotation) following one or more axes independently. So, a 3D object that can be translated along each of the three axes of a reference has three DoF, if it can also carry out rotations along the three axes then it will have an additional three DoF linked to rotation, so in total six DoF. In computing, it is possible to extend this concept to homotheties that are applied to 3D objects. Therefore, it is possible to work with nine DoF.

## 2.4.2. *3D selection/manipulation and navigation interactions*

Many types of interactions exist between a user and his/her machine. In Chapter 1, we saw that in the Geospace program, one had to pass through no fewer than 11 steps with 10 dialog boxes in order to create a cube, representing a total of 105 clicks or presses on the keyboard. This may be interesting from a teaching point of view in a formal construction (and this remains to be proven) but is not so for a student who cannot apprehend such a complex use of a program. We can therefore consider that there are 105 interactions here with the program, each one implying a visual return to the user. Tablets allow for interactions that are often qualified as more intuitive as we shall now see.

Navigation and selection/manipulation of 3D objects can take place with different techniques that depend on the technology used. On last generation tablets, there are three main types of materials used in these interactions: touchscreen surfaces, sensors (accelerometer, gyroscope) and cameras.

### 2.4.2.1. *3D interactions using a touchscreen*

In the use of modeling, animation and 3D rendering software, such as Blender[©] for example, one can legitimately expect to find widgets (see Figure 2.24) in order to interact with the software and move 3D objects. During the 1980s, two studies were carried out to develop modern widgets as they are found nowadays in software such as Blender[©].

Although these studies used a mouse as their entry system, they seem relevant here. From them, Bier introduced the concept of "Skitters and Jacks" [BIE 86]. "Skitters" correspond to 3D cursors that define a 3D position and orientation in the scene. Movements of the Skitters can be limited to an axis or a plane. The "Jacks", on the other hand, correspond to small references that the user can place throughout the scene in order to facilitate object assembly or to position new objects (see Figure 2.25). A few years later, Bier showed the benefits of adding a magnetic effect in a new study [BIE 90]. Still during the 1980s, Nielson and Olsen defined a widget corresponding to a small reference, close to what is found in Blender© nowadays (see Figure 2.24 (a)). In 1986, Nielson and Olsen [NIE 86] defined a technique named Triad Mouse that allowed the specification of 3D points through the projection of a movement of the mouse on to a map of the main axes of an object. They therefore suggest portioning the representation plane including the widget into six zones (see Figure 2.26 (a)). This limits the movement of the axis belonging to the interaction zone. The second idea from their proposal is to take advantage of the elementary geometrical elements that make up the object. In this way, it is possible to restrict movements to an axis or a plane by selecting two points, respectively, on an edge and a face (see Figure 2.26(b)).

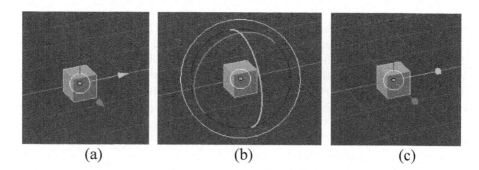

(a)                    (b)                    (c)

**Figure 2.24.** *Widgets used in Blender© to apply elementary transformations to objects: a) translation; b) rotation; c) scaling. For a color version of this figure, see www.iste.co.uk/bertolo/geometry.zip*

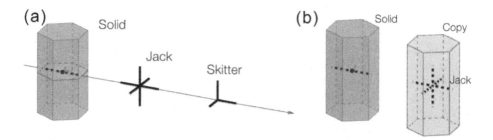

**Figure 2.25.** *Skitters and Jacks [BIE 86]: a) movement of a skitter along an axis and jack placement; b) positioning of copies of the solids on the jacks*

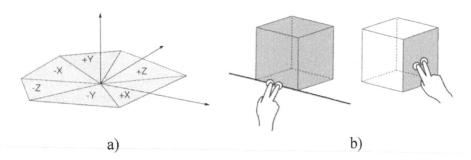

**Figure 2.26.** *Nielson and Olsen et al. [NIE 86] manipulation technique: a) partition of the representation plane including the widget into six zones; b) use of characteristic elements of the solid to restrict or define transformations. (CC BY SA 2.0, Gestureworks. See http://gestureworks.com)*

The apparition of popular touchscreens and the problems we have just described regarding the imprecision of fingers as well as gestures designed in order not to overload the screen with menus lead to the evolution of widgets. Schmidt *et al.* [SCH 08] developed the concept of transitory widgets that are called by the movement of a finger on the screen and depending on the context (see Figure 2.27). To mitigate the imprecision of fingers, widgets automatically orient themselves in a certain way to have a sufficiently large contact surface.

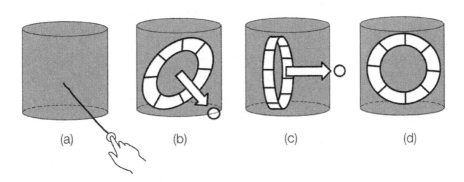

**Figure 2.27.** *Transitory widget [SCH 08]: a) invocation of the widget by moving a finger on the screen; b) apparition of the widget with an orientation corresponding to that of the finger movement on the screen; c) orientation of the crown in order to have a larger contact zone; d) disappearance of the translation arrow when the operation is impossible. (CC BY SA 2.0, Gestureworks. See http://gestureworks.com)*

Similarly, Cohé *et al.* designed the tBox, a widget that manages translations, rotations and scaling [COH 11]. The tBox is represented by a wire cuboid with parts of the edges of the same color wherever they are parallel (see Figure 2.28(a)) and inspired by the Maya software. Translations are carried out by touching an edge, which creates a cursor (see Figure 2.28(b)). Moving this cursor moves the object along the pre-determined axis. Rotations are carried out by making a movement perpendicular to an edge with a finger (see Figure 2.28(c)). Finally, scaling is carried out using two fingers. If both fingers "push" on either side of the widget, the scaling is uniform (see Figure 2.28(d)). If they are both positioned on opposite edges of a same face, the scaling is carried out parallel to the non-selected edges of the face (see Figure 2.28(d)).

The use of widgets is interesting as we can specify the transformation to be carried out as well as its characteristics or constraints (axis, plane, etc.). What is more, widgets are integrated into 3D vision and/or the object itself and they avoid the use of menus and decrease the search for information in the interface.

Widgets, however, also have some drawbacks in a 3D geometry learning context during the third primary cycle as well as in middle school. In the previously mentioned studies, several limitations in our chosen context can be noted:

1) all these studies were carried out on adults who have already developed a stable spatial representation rather than a developing one, unlike the students;

2) younger students still do not have fine enough motor skills, which increases the problems with precision linked to selection using a finger;

3) the addition of a widget to a solid has two main education drawbacks;

i) it complicates the acquisition of the topographical separation relationship in the younger students of our chosen age range [PIA 48],

ii) it complicates the cognitive deconstruction process of a 3D geometric object into figural units [DUV 05].

In the case of the tBox, the principle is very interesting where the chosen solid is a cuboid. In the cases where it is not a cuboid, either it is encompassed in the tBox or the tBox is positioned partially within the solid (as shown in Figure 2.28 (a)). In this case, the student must distinguish between the edges of the tBox and those of the solid, creating a possible confusion and thereby increasing the student's cognitive charge rather than diminishing it. This increase in the cognitive charge is not necessarily linked to the manipulation of the object but to the discovery of the solid and its characteristics: number of vertices, edges and faces.

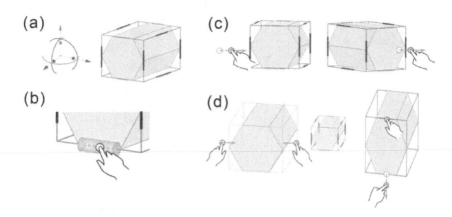

**Figure 2.28.** *Cohé et al's tBox. [COH 11]: a) presentation of the tBox and the Maya widget; b) translation technique; c) rotation technique; d) scaling technique. (CC BY SA 2.0, Gestureworks. See http://gestureworks.com)*

In the studies by Schmidt *et al.* followed by those of Cohé *et al.*, movements were used to call the widget and carry out a rotation. The use of these movements remains associated with widgets. Furthermore, the vast majority of the actions carried out with widgets only use a single point of contact (except for scaling with tBox). Currently, a large proportion of tablets are multi-touch. Many studies also focused on the use of such movements outside of widgets, while using several points of contact to move 3D objects on touchscreen surfaces.

Based on their 2006 work on 2D rotation and translation interactions on touchscreen tablets [HAN 06], Hancock *et al.* [HAN 07] launched in 2007 a shallow depth 3D interaction technique (of limited depth) involving the use of either one, two or three fingers. This technique uses the RNT (Rotation'N Translation) algorithm described by Kruger *et al.* [KRU 05]. The technique is as follows: with a single finger, only translations are carried out; with two, rotations around the Z-axis take place (see Figure 2.29); with three (using two hands), rotations around the two other axes take place.

Following this, in 2009, Hancock *et al.* introduced Sticky Tools, an interaction that manages six DoF (three DoF in translation and three DoF in rotation) as well as the use of a gravity simulation in the chosen 3D environment [HAN 09]. The interaction technique used in Sticky Tools is the Shallow Depth [HAN 07] that makes use of one to three fingers; to this is added the pinching/spreading of two fingers to lift an object from the chosen environment. When the object is "released", it falls to the ground thanks to the simulated gravity. All of Hancock's work has been carried out on touchscreen tables.

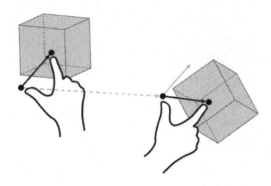

**Figure 2.29.** *Shallow Depth 3D interaction [HAN 07],*
*translation and rotation around the Z-axis using two fingers.*
*(CC BY SA 2.0, Gestureworks. See http://gestureworks.com)*

Based on the fact that rotation, scaling and translation (RST) interactions are now a standard in 2D, Reisman *et al.* [REI 09] suggested extending the principles used in 2D to 3D. The principle is to use three fingers to define a rotation or four to change a point of view (see Figure 2.30(b)). In the case of rotations, two fingers are used to define the axis of rotation and the third is used to carry it out. This technique, however, has the downside of having rotation cases where the axis definition is ambiguous, for example in the case where the three fingers form an equilateral triangle (see Figure 2.30(a))

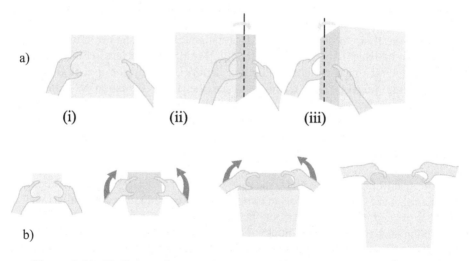

**Figure 2.30.** *3D Screen-Space RST technique from Reisman et al. [REI 09]:*
*a) ambiguity on the axis of rotation when the three fingers form an equilateral*
*triangle; b) switching perspectives using four fingers*

One of the main downsides to the RST interaction techniques that can carry out three simultaneous transformations is that it is difficult to carry out, for instance, a translation and an increase in size without introducing an unwanted rotation. Based on this, Nacenta *et al.* [NAC 09] showed the advantage of separating the 2D spatial manipulations. Martinet *et al.* [MAR 10a] extended this work into 3D by suggesting a DS3 (depth-separated screen space) technique, based on the separation of translation and rotation. The distinction between rotations and translations is made based on the number of contact points as well as the direct or indirect nature of the contact. Contact is direct if the point of contact is on the object being moved and indirect in the opposite case. In the case of a direct point of contact, colocation is also a used term, benefiting selection as Kin *et al.* [KIN 09] showed, although contributing to the masking of the screen. In the case of indirect contact, movement of a small object is facilitated by decreasing screen masking.

Martinet *et al.* [MAR 11] also suggested two interactive techniques for positioning 3D objects. As we have just seen, one of these is the Z-technique that allows the user to position an object in space. It is a two-handed operation composed of a direct contact on the object to carry out planar translations defined by the X- and Y-axes, followed by an indirect contact carried out with the second hand and of which the vertical movements allow the control of the object along the Z-axis (see Figure 2.31). Finally, the second technique is based on the principle of four views, used in modeling software such as Blender© and Maya©. This system was developed in order to make full use of the multi-touch function. Indeed, direct contact with a view moves the object through translation and the second hand indicates by pointing to the chosen location where the object is "teleported" to, instantly moving it to the desired location.

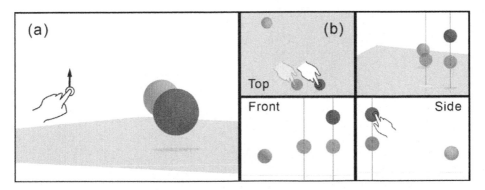

**Figure 2.31.** *3D positioning techniques from [MAR 10]:*
*a) Z-technique; b) extension of the four view system. (CC BY SA 2.0,*
*Gestureworks. See http://gestureworks.com)*

DS3 uses the Z-technique, which was also introduced by Martinet *et al.* [MAR 10b]. They compared their technique, DS3, with two of those already described, *Sticky Tools* from Hancock *et al.* and *Screen-Space* from Reisman *et al.* This comparison concluded that the separation of DoF increases the ease and performance of the interactions [MAR 10a].

All of Martinet *et al.*'s work was developed using touchscreen tables.

In a study about the creation of a virtual vegetal construction software by Pixar, Kin *et al.* [KIN 11] used a multi-touch table in order to try and simplify the construction process. They developed a group of movements (see Figure 2.33) used to position each object and thereby manage nine DoF. Their work defined several principles in the design of interactive movements which are as follows:

– the use of simple gestures for frequent operations;

– the use of a double joint contact (see Figure 2.32) to remove ambiguity from two similar operations, for example rotations around the Z-axis in the world-reference and in the reference of the object;

– to carry out only one operation at a time;

– to spread contacts over both hands;

– to use at most two fingers on each hand;

– to not assign one hand to a particular task;

– gesture movement must reflect the operation;

– to combine direct and indirect movements;

– to control at most two spatial parameters at once.

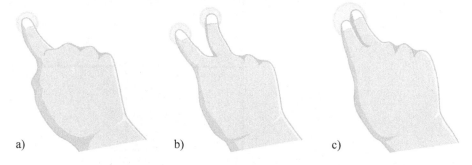

a)                              b)                              c)

**Figure 2.32.** *Different uses of two fingers on the same hand from Kin et al.'s [KIN 11] language of movements: a) one contact; b) two contacts with two fingers; c) a double joint contact using two fingers*

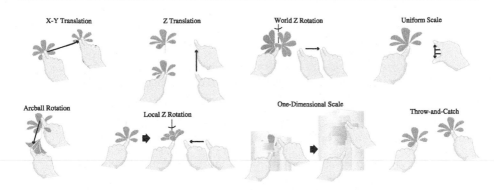

**Figure 2.33.** *All of Kin et al.'s [KIN 11] movements*

Finally, based on the fact that the vast majority of studies on interactive movements of 3D objects were carried out on touchscreen tables, Liu *et al.* [LIU 12] suggested a one-handed interactive technique using only two independent direct or indirect contacts (see Figure 2.34), managing six DoF (three DoF through translation and three DoF through rotation). Indeed, the use of interactions requiring three or more fingers and/or the use of both hands increases screen covering for these MDs.

We have seen many techniques allowing the movement of 3D objects using the screen of a multi-touch device. The majority of these techniques were developed on touchscreen tables where the dimensions did not limit certain of the movements that were harder to reproduce or adapt to touchscreen MDs.

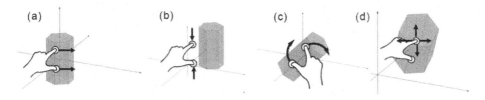

**Figure 2.34.** *Four movements managing the 6 DOF in Liu et al's technique: a) translation in X and Y; b) translation in Z; c) rotation around the Z-axis; d) rotation around other axes in the XY plane. (CC BY SA 2.0, Gestureworks. See http://gestureworks.com)*

### 2.4.2.2. 3D interactions using sensors

Nowadays, more and more MDs are equipped with sensors such as accelerometers, gyroscopes, GPS or digital compasses. All of these sensors allow the use of new selection, manipulation or navigation interactions in 3D. To begin, the following are the possibilities for each of these sensors:

– *accelerometer*: measures acceleration along the X-, Y- and Z-axes (see Figure 2.35(a)). Capable of detecting rotation and translation but not uniform movement as it is without acceleration;

– *gyroscope*: measures angular speed around the X-, Y- and Z-axes (see Figure 2.35(b)), therefore capable of detecting rotations but not translations;

– *GPS*: indicates geographic positioning of the MD but not orientation;

– *digital compass*: measures terrestrial magnetic field. Gives the orientation of the device.

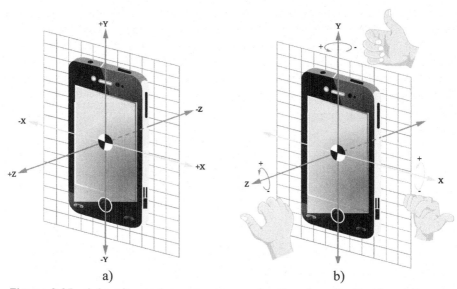

**Figure 2.35.** *a) Accelerometer measures acceleration along the X-, Y- and Z-axes; b) gyroscope measures the angular speed around the X-, Y- and Z-axes*

Baglioni *et al.* [BAG 09] categorized interactive movements on MDs, of which there are two types. The first type are impulsive and rapid movements of high acceleration. The second are fluid movements that are longer and have less acceleration. Some interactions such as *TimeTilt* [ROU 09] use a combination of impulsive and fluid movements, whereas others such as *Rock'n'Scroll* [BAR 00] only make use of fluid terminal inclination movements to navigate an image.

In 2000, Hinckley *et al.* [HIN 00] used an accelerometer to pivot the display of a Personal Digital Assistant (PDA) depending on its orientation. *MagiTact* [KET 10] moves documents from left to right, up and down, zooms into them and even accepts or refuses calls using a magnet and the smartphone's electronic compass. Ketabdar *et al.* [KET 10] used the magnetic perturbation induced by the magnet, which vary depending on its position as well as its proximity to define interactive movements in the space surrounding the smartphone. *TouchOver* [SCO 11] suggests a multimodal positioning and selection interaction that couples the accelerometer with a touchscreen. Positioning is carried out using the touchscreen and selection through the accelerometer by inclining the terminal. Although *TouchOver* can be used in a 3D environment, all the interactive techniques described above were actually developed for the 2D. Hürst and Helder [HUR 11] suggested the use of the accelerometer in the modification of points of view as well as a user's aim in a virtual 3D environment. Any modification is limited as the 3D environment is "glued" to the MD. Finally, Liang *et al.* [LIA 12] suggested coupling interactions using the touchscreen and sensors of an MD in order to manipulate 3D objects located on a large surface.

To conclude this brief section, there are several interesting tracks such as multimodality, which combines both sensor- and movement-based interactions with navigation possibilities, or at least the management of more "natural" points of view than the use of a joystick or a tactile interaction. Impulsive movements can also be excluded as they present too high a risk for children. Therefore, any interaction making use of sensors must be based on fluid movements.

### 2.4.2.3. *3D interactions using a camera*

Video cameras have almost become a standard of MDs. Whether smartphones or tablets, few are not equipped with them. Furthermore, mobile terminals have an increasing calculation power, approaching that of small laptops. Even if problems with image treatment and robustness of detection algorithms persist, it may be useful to explore tracks such as that of the camera as an interaction in 3D environments, be it to navigate or select and manipulate objects.

In 2005, Hachet *et al.* [HAC 05a] created an interactive technique using a camera and a tangible map to navigate and manipulate 3D objects. This technique is used to move around within large-scale maps in *TangiMap* [HAC 05b].

The use of a camera on MDs is often associated with the term augmented reality (AR). Henrysson *et al.* carried out a study on the positioning and manipulation of 3D objects in an AR scene [HEN 05]. Their technique makes use of a camera and an interface button as well as the movement of the AR marker. They carried out a comparative study using several variations of their interactive technique: with purely keyboard-based entries, mobile inclinations detected by the camera, tangible objects and the use of the second front-facing camera [HEN 07]. The results showed a preference for the use of tangible entries in translations and the use of the keypad for rotations.

In 2011, Francone and Nigay drew attention thanks to the i3D software [FRA 11]. It integrates an interaction technique based on face-tracking of the user, controlling the point of view of a 3D scene (see Figure 2.36).

With *PalmSpace*, Kratz *et al.* [KRA 12] used a depth camera to detect hand movements in order to rotate 3D objects. This technique combines the three DoF associated with the hand with the three DoF associated with the object rotation in order to mitigate the limits of 2D touchscreens. This interactive technique is itself limited by the previously mentioned psychological constraints (see Figure 2.25).

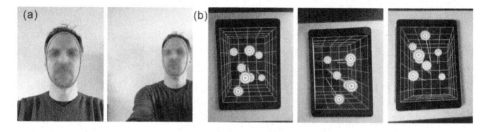

**Figure 2.36.** *i3D [FRA 11]: a) face-tracking; b) example use of the i3D software*

Finally, Fan *et al.* looked into new possibilities by coupling the already present camera and accelerometer in order to better detect 3D movements and therefore to be able, in the future, to define new manipulation interactions [FAN 12].

As we have just seen, the use of the camera can lead to new interactions. It does however, remain problematic in the detection of images, which is dependent on ambient lighting conditions. It is therefore useful to think about multimodal interactions using the camera that could mitigate these problems.

## 2.5. "Language" of interactions and classifications

We have seen that it is possible to use several different entry systems on MDs and that these allow the use of manipulation interactions in the 3D environment. It therefore seems useful to further study the categories of these interactions, and in particular the groups of movements such as those developed by Kin *et al.* [KIN 11]. Indeed, in this context, we must be able to manipulate 3D solids, but it must also be possible to add functionalities specific to teaching 3D geometry and the construction of special representation in students. If several movements must be carried out at the same time, it is therefore important to question these groups, languages and grammars of movements.

## 2.5.1. *Language and grammar of gestures*

As we have seen with Kin *et al.*'s group of interactions [KIN 11], from the moment that we wish to integrate interactions into everyday situations and associate them with a human activity, it is essential to think of them as a whole, even a language of interactions. In order to limit the cognitive surcharge linked to the complex learning of a language of gestures, these must be sufficiently intuitive. Therefore, if the gestures of basic transformations are sufficiently "natural", there will be no real learning needed, except in the cases of more complex manipulations, corresponding to more specific and less frequent situations. This implies the need to correctly identify the target consumers as well as any constraints and limits of the activity.

In this manner, Wobbrock *et al.* [WOB 09] carried out a study aiming to define a group of gestures for touchscreen surfaces (once more, here these were touchscreen tables) from movements suggested by users, by trying to identify the most "natural" of these. They identified 1080 movements carried out by 20 users and applied to 27 commands. These gestures were carried out with either one or two hands and with one or more points of contact. Figure 2.37 shows these movements. Wobbrock *et al.* highlighted several very important points which are as follows:

– the three authors only predicted 60.9% of the movements users suggested, highlighting the importance of including the user;

– there are no "obvious" movements: the final classification includes 57% of the user-suggested movements, with several suggested for each command (four propositions for zooming);

– the importance of the WIMP (Windows, Icons, Menus and Pointing) paradigm in users who often base themselves on it (72% of movements are adaptations of the mouse use).

Following this study, Cohé and Hachet [COH 12] studied 432 movements carried out by 16 participants. Their study shows, along with that of Wobbrock *et al.*, that there are no "natural" movements, or no "obvious" movements as such, particularly in the case of rotation. Indeed, authors present 10 different gestures for rotation and the most frequently used movement is only used 17.95% of the time.

They also present five different gestures for translation and six different gestures for scaling, the most frequently used movements are used at 34.75% and 36.57%, respectively.

It is also important to note that all of these studies were carried out on adults.

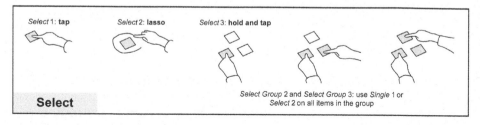

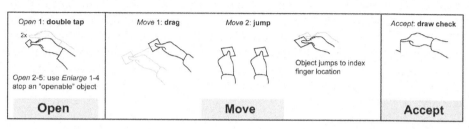

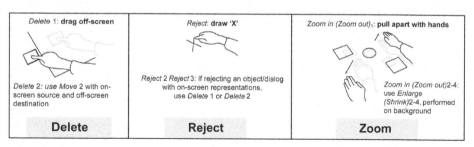

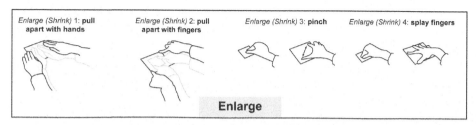

**Figure 2.37.** *Group of movements suggested by Wobbrock et al. after having studied 1080 propositions from 20 people for 27 commands [WOB 09]*

Hinrichs and Carpendale [HIN 11] studied both adult and child users in real situations of the use of a multi-touch informative table at the Vancouver Aquarium. Along with Wobbrock *et al.*, as well as Cohé and Hachet, they noted the use of different gestures for the same action. Their study highlighted the following interesting points:

– it is advised to map out several gestures for the same action (many-to-one) to improve the user experience;

– the choice of gestures is strongly influenced by the sequence of actions that has just been carried out. Indeed, the user chooses the gestures that are physically the easiest in the continuity of the sequence;

– they showed a social context for the gestures;

– the comparison of two samples of both adults and children showed differences in the following:

- low-level actions,

- gestures used,

- use of the "territory" of the table.

It is interesting to note that in this context, there is a difference between the gestures carried out by children and those carried out by adults. Hinrichs and Carpendale, among others, noted that children used more two-handed gestures than adults. Taking into account the idea of the continuous sequence of movements, we can assume that maturity differences for motor-skills are partly to blame for these differences in gestures.

Given the multitude of gestures and all the interactions still to come, Kammer *et al.* [KAM 10] formalized a definition of grammar. They first suggested separating the gestures into atomic elements (see Figure 2.38) and then defining a grammar using these elements in order to describe any type of gesture (see Figure 2.39).

Kammer *et al.* put forward that their grammar, named *GeForMT*, must be able to address all the intentions that the user wants to express through gestures on a tactile surface. For this, Kammer *et al.* took a semiotic approach that describes all phenomena associated with the production and interpretation of signals and symbols. The syntax describes the symbols and their combination, whereas the semantic relates to the meaning and the pragmatism to the user's mental model.

In parallel to this formalization of interactive gesture on a touchscreen, interaction classifications for MDs have evolved by including different technologies that became standards and linked interactions.

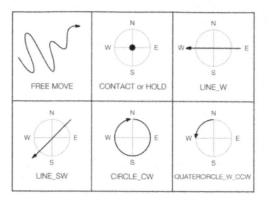

**Figure 2.38.** *Examples of atomic gestures in the grammar developed by [KAM 10]*

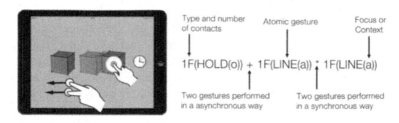

**Figure 2.39.** *Example of a complex gesture as described by the GeFormMT syntax (right) and the resulting movement (left). (CC BY SA 2.0, Gestureworks. See http://gestureworks.com)*

### 2.5.2. Classifications

There are many categorizations of interactions. This diversity is explained by the diversity of parameters that come into play such as the different types of users (adults, children, special need users, etc.), the different types of devices (computers, tactile, MD), the different entry (keyboard, microphone, sensor, touchscreen, multi-touch) and exit systems (screen, speaker, haptic feedback, etc.).

One classification of entry or exit interactive techniques on MDs was carried out by Roudaut and Lecolinet [ROU 07]. This classification also links the physical devices and corresponding interactive languages used (see Figure 2.40). Based on the classification of Roudaut *et al.* as well as that of Karam and Schraefel [KAR 05],

Baglioni *et al.* [BAG 09] developed a classification that takes into account currently available sensors on most MDs (see Figure 2.41). However, this classification does not take into account gestures on touchscreens.

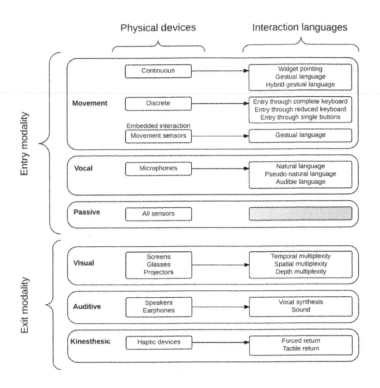

**Figure 2.40.** *Classification of Roudaut and [LEC 07] of entry and exit interaction techniques on mobile devices*

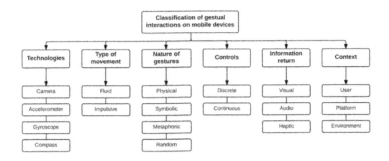

**Figure 2.41.** *Classification of gestual interactions using sensors from [BAG 09]*

Martinet *et al.* [MAR 10a] developed a classification of rotation and translation gestures in 3D, taking into account the number of contact points used as well as their type (direct, indirect). This classification was extended by Liu *et al.* [LIU 12] who integrated potential movement into the contacts (see Figure 2.42).

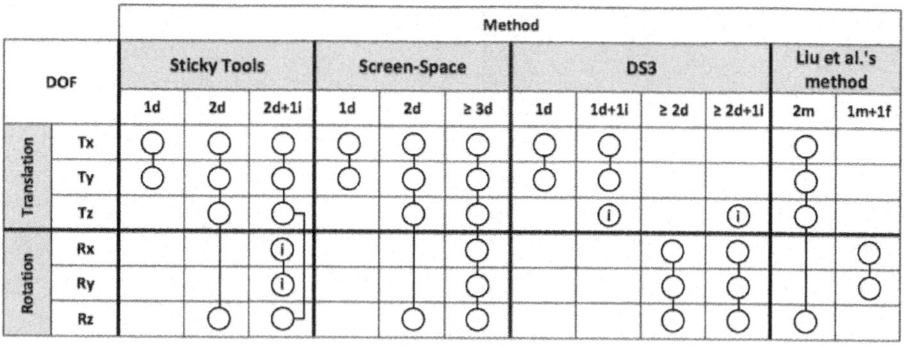

| DOF | | Method | | | | | | | | | | | |
|---|---|---|---|---|---|---|---|---|---|---|---|---|---|
| | | Sticky Tools | | | Screen-Space | | | DS3 | | | | Liu et al.'s method | |
| | | 1d | 2d | 2d+1i | 1d | 2d | ≥3d | 1d | 1d+1i | ≥2d | ≥2d+1i | 2m | 1m+1f |
| Translation | Tx | ○ | ○ | ○ | ○ | ○ | ○ | ○ | ○ | | | ○ | |
| | Ty | ○ | ○ | ○ | ○ | ○ | ○ | ○ | ○ | | | ○ | |
| | Tz | | ○ | ○ | | ○ | ○ | | (i) | | (i) | ○ | |
| Rotation | Rx | | | (i) | | | ○ | | | ○ | ○ | | ○ |
| | Ry | | | (i) | | | ○ | | | ○ | ○ | | ○ |
| | Rz | | ○ | ○ | | ○ | ○ | | | ○ | ○ | ○ | |

**Figure 2.42.** *Taxonomy from [MAR10] extended by [LIU 12] based on the number and type of contact (direct: d, indirect: i) then on the fact that the contact is in movement (m) or fixed (f)*

In this final classification, time was still not taken into account in order to further extend it and to take place in the interactions.

# 3

# Elaboration and Classification of Interactions

After having taught state of the art 3D geometry followed by human–computer interactions in the manipulation of 3D objects in our chosen learning context, we shall now explain our research procedure. In this chapter, we shall define our user-centered approach followed by a study on user habits and needs. Based on these results, we shall define our interaction choices and will formalize the grammar and language used to describe and meet the user's needs. We shall then present the categorization of the chosen interactions and will describe their evaluation on students within our chosen age range.

## 3.1. Human-centered design

Historically, the development of information systems was techno-centered and it remained up to the user to adapt to the technology. The slogan of the Universal Exhibition in 1933 summarizes this school of thought very accurately: "Science finds, industry applies, man conforms". As technology has evolved very fast, it has become increasingly difficult for man to adapt. The complexification of these systems led to an increase in the required learning and adaptation time for interfaces, as well as an increase in user mistakes, often provoking frustration and sometimes rejection. The development of HCI research has enabled the recalibration of the balance between the techno-centered and the enthno-centered visions. Several approaches have been therefore developed to take into account the user's needs and amongst these is human-centered design. Our study and the development of our software were based on this approach. We shall now define and outline its main principles.

### 3.1.1. *A definition*

The term human-centered design was first used by Norman *et al.* [NOR 86]. As the name indicates, here the user is placed at the center of the conception process. Norman's motto summarizes this spirit and goes completely against that of the Universal Exhibition: "People propose, science studies, technology conforms". This process has been the subject of several standards, of which the last dates from 2010 (standard ISO 9241-210), that defines it as follows:

> "2.7 *Human-centred design:* the approach to systems design and development that aims to make interactive systems more usable by focusing on the use of the system and applying human factors/ergonomics and usability knowledge and techniques.
>
> Note 1 to entry: The term "human-centred design" is used rather than "user-centred design" in order to emphasize that this part of ISO 9241 also addresses impacts on a number of stakeholders, not just those typically considered as users. However, in practice, these terms are often used synonymously.
>
> Note 2 to entry: Usable systems can provide a number of benefits, including improved productivity, enhanced user well-being, avoidance of stress, increased accessibility and reduced risk of harm.
> [...]
>
> 2.13 *Usability:* the extent to which a system, product or service can be used by specified users to achieve specified goals with effectiveness, efficiency and satisfaction in a specified context of use."

For Oviatt [OVI 06], human-centered design "advocates that a more promising and enduring approach is to model users' natural behavior to begin with, including any constraints on their ability to attend, learn, and perform, so that interfaces can be designed that are more intuitive, easier to learn, and freer of performance errors".

### 3.1.2. *Principles of the user-based approach*

The ISO 9241-210 standard defines the main principles of this process:

1) design is based on an explicit understanding of the user, the tasks and the environment;

2) users are involved in the design and development;

3) the process is iterative;

4) design involves the whole of the user experience;

5) the design team includes competency parameters as well as multidisciplinary points of view.

According to Oviatt [OVI 06], one of the themes common to all discussions about the principles of human-centered design, its strategies, illustrations and research results is the cognitive load, and more precisely how to minimize any excess of this due to the use of an interface.

In this context, Oviatt suggested eight main principles in the design of an interface:

1) to make use of user experience, knowledge and types of behavior and to adapt to their behavior and preferences;

2) to support multimodal, natural and flexible communication models;

3) to guide, in a transparent way, the user-entries in order to minimize the difficulties linked to variability linguistics and behavior, as well as reduce system errors and improve usability;

4) to minimize the cognitive load associated with the planning of user-entries;

5) to take into account user work practices rather than change them;

6) to support representation systems that the user needs within the interface;

7) to minimize the cognitive load associated with surplus complexity associated with the exit system (useless functionalities that can distract attention during the task);

8) to minimize interruptions that stop the user from engaging in a high level of planning, thinking and problem solving.

Based on these principles, we shall now describe the approach taken during our study.

Firstly, an analysis was carried out on user needs and behaviors, corresponding to the first human-centered design principles of standard ISO 9241-210 as well as points (1) and (5). This study began with the evaluation of pre-existing 3D geometry software. Then, focus groups were organized alongside interviews with students of primary and middle school age, teachers from both cycles, as well as with students and trainers from the (Institut Universitaire de Formation des Maîtres (IUFM) replaced in 2013 by the École Supérieure du Professorat et de l'Éducation). As specified by point (3) of standard ISO 9241-210, our process is iterative. This study allowed us to develop the first categorization of interactions depending on functionalities used in 3D geometry software used in teaching.

## 3.2. Study of the needs and behaviors of users

### 3.2.1. *Study of pre-existing 3D geometry software*

In order to carry out our study on pre-existing 3D geometry software, we studied *Geospace*, *Cabri-3D* and *Calque 3D*. Obviously, other programs exist such as *Série 3D* or *Ateliers de géométrie 3D*. There are also those that initially specialized in 2D geometry and that offer modules in 3D geometry, for example *CaRMetal* and *GeoGebra*. The latter two were rapidly removed from our study, as the first requires the installation of macros (not enabling students' comprehension) and the second was only available as a beta version at the time, and only became available in the autumn of 2014. From this date, *GeoGebra* was available for desktop and tablet but the specificities of tablets, such as the multi-touch function, were not fully accounted for. Amongst the software aimed specifically at 3D geometry, we chose:

– *Geospace*, as it is the only 3D geometry software that is suggested in the list of those authorized by CAPES mathematics and therefore accessible to future middle school mathematics teachers;

– *Cabri-3D*, due to the numerous studies carried out on it [CHA 97, MIT 10];

– *Calque 3D*, due to the fact that its development led to a PhD thesis [VAN 99] regarding the user as a teacher in the conception of *enseignement intelligent assisté par ordinateur* or intelligent computer-assisted teaching.

The three chosen programs were developed for desktop use and therefore correspond to the Windows, Icons, Menus and Pointing device or WIMP paradigm.

Thus, most of the actions are carried out through the use of menus that are relatively complex and difficult to learn for third cycle middle school students (Figure 3.1). One other limitation linked to desktop use, described in Chapter 1, is the fact that the observer cannot move around in order to modify his or her point of view. These three programs clearly allow the user to do this through the use of different projections. However, the problem of "seeing" the scene move on the screen rather than the user "seeing" by moving remains, although for a student, this corresponds to two separate tasks in the context of spatial structuring. Based on these observations, we shall firstly and briefly compare the actions required to create two simple polyhedrons. Secondly, we shall compare the translation and rotation actions, both of which are basic transformations in the manipulation of 3D environments. Thirdly, we shall compare the possibilities of working on nets that are more specific to 3D geometry teaching. These different tasks were chosen as they correspond to the requirements of middle school, and would need to be completed in the context of the mathematical curriculum.

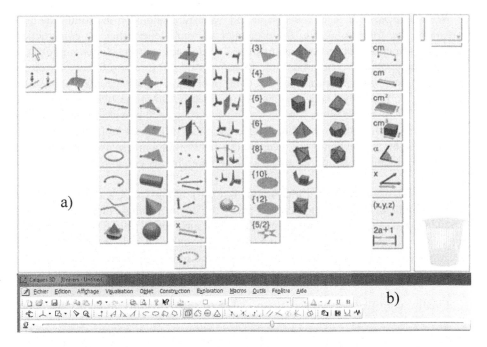

**Figure 3.1.** *Interfaces of the two programs: a) Cabri-3D; b) Calque 3D*

As we have already seen in the previous chapters, using the *Geospace* program to create a cube requires 11 steps with 10 dialog boxes and a total of 105 clicks or keyboard touches. The creation of a cuboid requires 97 interactions throughout nine dialog boxes. *Geospace* does not let the user directly create a cube or polyhedron, implying the use of a vector product or the creation of a plane in order to define one. Using *Cabri-3D*, the creation of a cube requires four interactions and a cuboid five interactions. *Cabri-3D* allows the direct creation of a cube or polyhedron, explaining the smaller number of steps compared with *Geospace*. Finally, with *Calque 3D*, the creation of a cube requires 10 interactions and a polyhedron 70 interactions. This software allows the direct creation of a cube but not a cuboid, explaining the difference in the number of interactions between these two solids.

After having explained the brief creation of two basic solids, we shall study the possibilities of transformation in terms of translations and rotations allowed by the software. In cases where the transformation can be carried out based on mouse interactions on the solid, the interaction is *direct*; whereas in the opposite cases where the interaction requires the use of menus and dialog boxes, followed by the keyboard and/or the mouse, this is called a *parametric interaction*.

With *Geospace*, the user is unable to carry out translations on the solid. The user can move the free points, i.e. those created without dependency or construction constraints (a construction constraint can be an intersection point, for example). It is possible to pivot the scene around the three axes of the screen reference by direct interaction but only 2 degrees of freedom (DoF) are simultaneously accessible. *Geospace*, on the other hand, does not allow direct rotation through a single solid. Although it is possible rotate a solids' along a particular axis within *Geospace*, the action remains difficult and implies the creation of a real variable (angle), to be manipulated by the keyboard, followed by the creation of a macro using this variable and by re-drawing the solid for each new value taken by the variable.

*Cabri-3D* software allows translations but only along the X and Y axes of the world-reference. It is also possible to pivot the scene through direct interactions around the two axes (two simultaneous DoF) but surprisingly, these two axes do not belong to the same reference. Indeed, the first rotation axis is the Y axis in the world-reference and the second is the X axis in the screen reference. Furthermore, it is impossible to manipulate a solid by rotating it in order to simply observe it.

Finally, with *Calque 3D* it is not possible to move a solid through translation. *Calque 3D* allows scene rotation through direct interaction along the X and Y axes in the screen reference. However, moving the scene through rotations by using two simultaneous DoF requires the "3D rendering" mode (Figure 3.2). Using this mode, it is possible to manipulate the scene independently from the creation window. However, rotation of a single solid is not possible.

Even if the scene contains several solids, none of the three programs allows the manipulation of the solids independently from each other. So, either these programs were designed to only show one solid at a time, or to manage scenes as a whole. In both cases, this limits the manipulation and observation possibilities for the user.

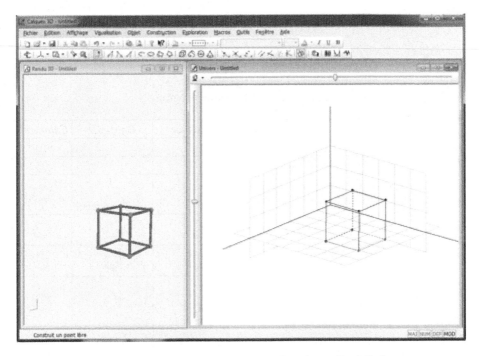

**Figure 3.2.** *Calque 3D with the two boxes: on the left, the 3D rendering box and on the right the creation window*

Only *Geospace* and *Cabri-3D* allow nets to be created. These can then be moved around like any other solid. For *Geospace*, one must create a real variable and use it in a dialog box. Opening or closing of the net is then controlled using the keyboard. It is also interesting to note than the initial solid remains visible when the pattern is opened up (Figure 3.3 (a)). In the case of *Cabri-3D*, creation takes place using a button on the menu followed by a direct interaction on one of the vertices of the solid that defines the degree to which the solid net is either opened or closed. The initial solid is therefore no longer visible and only the net remains (Figure 3.3 (b)). Neither of the two programs allows the modification of the pattern.

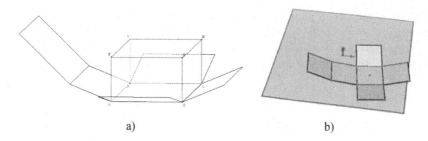

a)                                              b)

**Figure 3.3.** *Representation of the nets: a) with Geospace; b) with Cabri-3D.*

Table 3.1 summarizes the analysis of the three programs.

| | *Geospace* | *Cabri-3D* | *Calque 3D* |
|---|---|---|---|
| Creation of a cube (number of interactions) | 105 | 4 | 10 |
| Creation of a cuboid (number of interactions) | 97 | 5 | 70 |
| Translation in the oxy plane (2 DoF) by direct interaction/reference used | ✖ | ✔ world reference | ✖ |
| Translation in another plane (2 DoF) | ✖ | ✖ | ✖ |
| Translation in space (3 DoF) by direct interaction | ✖ | ✖ | ✖ |
| Rotation of a single solid of the scene through parametric interaction / number of DoF / type of interaction | ✔ 1 DoF parametric | ✖ | ✖ |
| Number of possible axes of rotation of the scene / reference used | 3 axes, screen reference | 2 axes, 1 axis as a screen reference and 1 axis from the world one | 2 axes, screen reference |
| Number of maximal simultaneous DoF in the scene rotation | 2 DoF, direct interaction | 2 DoF, direct interaction | 2 DoF, direct interaction |
| Observer's point of view taken into account | ✖ | ✖ | ✖ |
| Generation of the net of a polyhedron | ✔ | ✔ | ✖ |
| Dynamic management of the degree to which the pattern can be opened / type of interaction | ✔ parametric | ✔ direct | ✖ |
| Possibility of modifying the net | ✖ | ✖ | ✖ |

**Table 3.1.** *Analysis and comparison of three 3D geometry programs*

### 3.2.2. *Study of users' behaviors and needs*

After having carried out a comparative study on several points of three pre-existing 3D geometry programs, we carried out interviews with their potential users. The aim was to identify the habits and practices of the software users, as well as any shortfalls and possible areas of development. In this context, we only carried out our interviews with a section of the potential users: teachers or future teachers. They were carried out in two parts and under two different modalities: semi-directive interviews or focus groups.

#### 3.2.2.1. *User interviews*

Semi-directive interviews were carried out with 28 potential users, made up of the following:

– six school teachers (first degree);

– 11 future teachers (trainees in CAPES mathematics);

– eight middle school teachers (second degree);

– three IUFM mathematical trainers.

The interviews were based on the use of 3D geometry programs and highlighted the following points:

– the students of 23 teachers out of the 28 do not use these programs. Seven do not use them at all and 16 use them only as a support to illustrate their lessons (Figure 3.4). Furthermore, the 23 teachers whose students do not use the programs justify this through the complexity of their use, which is too high for their classes, but would not exclude the possibility of using them with high school students. Of the 23 teachers who were resistant to the use of this software by the students, seven never use them in the classroom even if they are able to use them, arguing logistical problems or inappropriateness in their level of teaching, mainly the case in school teachers (Figure 3.4).

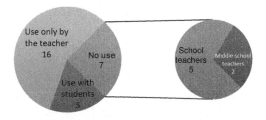

**Figure 3.4.** *Distribution of the use of 3D geometry software by teachers*

All the teachers interviewed highlighted the need for a learning period in the use of these programs, which was found to be long and fastidious by 20 of these teachers, the majority of which used *Geospace*. Indeed, several of these users also highlighted their struggles with manipulating the representations of the solids by using a mouse: "it never really goes where you want it", "it is difficult to place the figure correctly". These remarks partially explain the lack of willingness of the teachers to let their students use the programs.

Twenty-six teachers out of 28 thought that these programs still were beneficial in the teaching of 3D geometry and that they allowed students to "see better".

Twenty-one of the teachers regretted not being able to create different nets or being able to modify them, with the programs only creating one pattern per solid.

During these sessions, the teachers also highlighted several existing or missing functionalities that seemed important to them:

– the possibilities of dynamic scaling of solids which characterize these programs. Whatever the transformations applied to the solid, the program conserves its mathematical properties and therefore a cube will always remain a cube, a cuboid a cuboid, etc.;

– the possibility of modifying nets in order to create new ones;

– the possibility of manipulating the solids individually;

– the possibility of "easily" studying sections of the solid through the use of a plane, this functionality being put forward only by middle school teachers as it corresponds to teaching in Year 10.

Following these interviews, our study and the state of the art in interactions, we put forward a first classification based on the expected functionalities.

### 3.2.2.2. *First categorizations*

Once all the main functionalities were defined, we mapped them with interactions, trying to keep an overall view defining a group of interactions that are both coherent and without ambiguity. In our context, it is not enough to be able to carry out a translation with 3 DoF or to find a better gesture for the rotation of a solid. Not only do gestures need to be "easily" and "quickly" assimilated, but they must also take place in a group that will meet the needs of the users. We have therefore attempted to take into account the following tasks:

– selecting a solid;

– applying a translation (2 and 3 DoF);

– applying a rotation to a solid independently from the others;

– changing the point of view/ position of the observer;

– generating a net and modifying it;

– scaling a solid, dynamically, by conserving its mathematical properties;

– sectioning a solid through a plane and being able to separate it into two independent solids;

– creating a solid;

– deleting a solid;

– assembling two solids;

– changing color.

We then created a heuristic card showing an initial classification based on the functionalities highlighted by the users (Figure 3.5). In order to ensure coherence between the interactions that are coupled with needs, we created a second heuristic card that represents a second classification based on interactions and taking into account the number of contacts as well as their directivity (direct or indirect) (Figure 3.6).

Based on these two classifications (Figures 3.5 and 3.6), we developed a prototype and during a focus group recorded their opinions, thereby taking an iterative approach as prescribed by point (3) of standard ISO 9241-210 and points (5) and (6) of Oviatt's recommendations [OVI 06].

### 3.2.2.3. Focus group with users

Taking advantage of the Sésamath group General Assembly, covering all mathematics teachers in collaborative projects based on the use of Technologies de l'Information et de la Communication pour l'Enseignement (TICE or Information and Communication Technologies for Teaching), we held a focus group with 11 teachers: eight from middle school and three from primary.

We split the focus group into three sections:

– *section one*: we covered all of the main sections of the interviews in order to gather feedback from the teachers regarding the use of 3D geometry programs and what they should be;

– *section two*: presentation of the prototype and developing functionalities;

– *section three*: exchanges around the presentation and links between primary and middle school.

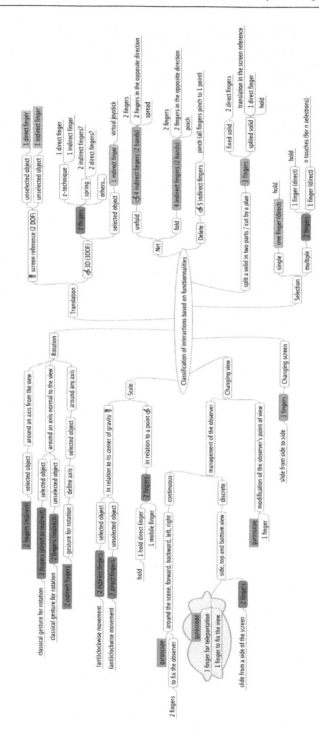

**Figure 3.5.** *Initial classification based on functionalities suggested by the users and our state of the art*

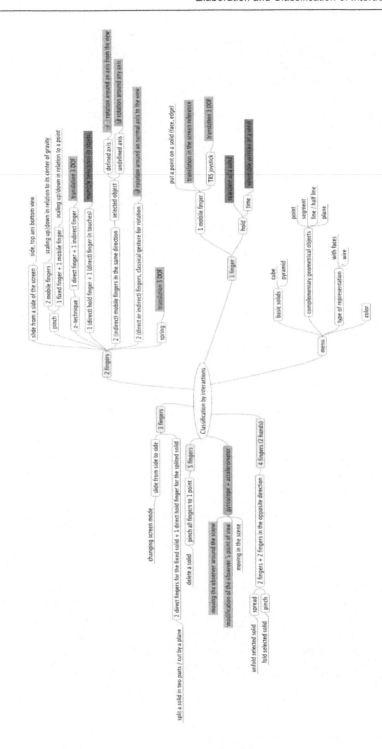

**Figure 3.6.** *Second classification based on interactions and the number of contacts and directivity*

Initially, the same remarks were suggested as during our first interviews with the users (see section 2.2.1). Primary teachers added only that it would be interesting to have several views of a solid: full, full with the edges and vertices visible, and the "solid's skeleton" (wire representation).

In the second section, we presented our prototype that would allow the following:

– selection of the solid;

– translation with 2 DoF;

– rotation in a solid, independently from all others, following either 1 or 3 DoF;

– change in the observer's position around the scene;

– generation of a net for the solid, with the possibility of dynamically modifying the degree of opening.

Followed by the functionalities being developed:

– translation with 3 DoF;

– the possibility of modifying a net;

– the possibility of assembling solids as long as these possess at least one identical face, in form and dimensions;

– the use of physical solids (tangible) for the creation of solids in the program.

The group members then tested the prototype in order to give some initial qualitative feedback on the interactions. After use, the teachers found the prototype to be "simple" and easily comprehended. The initial reactions were positive and the presentation led to the following feedback:

– The possibility of rotating the solid along 1 DoF around an axis defined by the two vertices of a solid was presented. The primary school teachers did not see the use of this functionality.

– The assembly of the solid was judged to be secondary to the tasks. For middle school teachers, this was seen as useful for several observations but within the margin of their usual behaviors. Primary school teachers, however, found this to be an interesting functionality but only for cubes, in order to develop the notion of volume through the assembly of several smaller cubes to compare the volume obtained through assembly and that already available.

– The use of duplicating a solid thereby became apparent.

In the third section, several propositions emerged:

– the possibility of duplicating a solid;

– the possibility of printing a solid on a plane ("floor of the scene");

– modifications of the color of the solid and that of its faces, edges and vertices;

– the possibility of creating a net based on "for example a face distributor" rather than needing to modify a pre-existing one, which "is not the same task for the student!";

– middle-school teachers closely studied the possibility of creating sections of a solid through a plane, with the possibility of studying each resulting solid independently.

After having studied the pre-existing programs as well as the habits and needs of a section of the future users, we developed functionalities as well as the modalities chosen to carry them out. These go further than tactile interactions with the screen, as we have already outlined our desire to better take advantage of the pre-existing technological solutions in tactile devices, with the aim of better meeting the expectations of users.

## 3.3. Our grammar and interaction language

After having taken into account the needs and habits of program users, as well as the different theoretical references of the state of the art, we fixed a group of interactions that would allow the program to meet all expectations. Certain associated functionalities and interactions led to the exploration of several paths, such as translations, that we will describe later on. The improvement of our first classification led to the extension of the taxonomy suggested by [MAR 11], followed by the definition of a grammar and language for the interactions. Finally, in parallel to this, a prototype was developed in order to evaluate these suggestions.

### 3.3.1. Classification of tactile movement interactions

We suggest a new classification that completes [MAR 11]'s taxonomy, which was based on that of [CAR 91]. [MAR 11] suggested taking into account the number of contacts, directivity (direct or indirect contact) as well as the type of manipulation (integral and separable) in their taxonomy. In an effort to simplify the taxonomy, the authors did not introduce any notations to represent the gestures. We therefore suggest extending it with the aim of classifying the inherent gestures in the use of 3D geometry programs in a learning situation [BER 13c]. It was necessary to introduce other notation to manage the new variables:

– *selection*: in a scene made up of several elements, the fact that an object is in a binary state of either selected or non-selected allows the manipulation of target solids.

– *mobility*: [MAR 11]'s taxonomy does not say whether the contacts are moving or not, whereas in this study, stationary direct contact and moving direct contact are considered two different interactions.

– *time*: in many programs, long contact is found to be a means of interaction (often to make a contextual menu appear). This notion of time is absent from the initial taxonomy and is an element we have chosen to include here.

The composition of the number of contacts, their directivity, the type of manipulation, the mobility of selection and time all enrich the interaction modes as defined by [MAR 11]. For each mode, an interaction possibility and/or the management of a DoF is represented by a *circle* when the solid is not selected and by a *square* when it is. When a movement allows the manipulation of an object following several DoF, the circles or squares are linked by a line. The letters *d, i, f* and *m* signify, respectively, the terms direct, indirect, fixed and mobile. Finally, when a minimum time is required to carry out an interaction, we indicate this within the circle or square. So, for instance, "*1df + 2im*" indicates a fixed direct contact and two indirect mobile contacts. Table 3.2 is a representation of this taxonomy applied to our interaction language.

| | | Interaction mode | | | | | | | |
|---|---|---|---|---|---|---|---|---|---|
| | | 1d | | 1i | | 2dm | 2im | 1df + 2im | 2im + 2im |
| | | f | m | f | m | | | | |
| Selection | | (0,5) | | | | | | | |
| De-selection | | | | [0,5] | | | | | |
| Translation | Tx | | ◯ | | | | | ☐ | |
| | Ty | | ◯ | | | | | ☐ | |
| | Tz | | | | | | | ☐ | |
| Rotation | Rx | | | | | | | ☐ | |
| | Ry | | | | | | | ☐ | |
| | Rz | | | | | | | ☐ | |
| Net | | | | | | | | | ☐ |
| Duplication | | | | | | | | ☐ | |
| Assembly | | | | | | ◯ | | | |
| Deletion | | | ◯ | | | | | | |

**Table 3.2.** *Classification of tactile interactions depending on the number of contacts, their directivity, mobility and duration*

In order to define our language of gestural interactions more formally, we have defined a grammar based on the extended Backus-Naur form (EBNF: ISO/IEC 14977: 1996(E)) and inspired by the *GeForMT* grammar [KAM 10]. Following this, we present our language of interactions using this grammar.

### 3.3.2. *Definition of the grammar*

In the EBNF, the following characters represent operators (by order of increasing importance):

| | |
|---|---|
| * | repetition |
| - | absence |
| , | concatenation |
| \| | choice |
| = | definition |
| ; | termination |

Normal priority is overridden by the following pairs of punctuation:

| | | |
|---|---|---|
| ' | first quotation | ' |
| " | second quotation | " |
| (* | comment | *) |
| ( | group | ) |
| [ | optional group | ] |
| { | repeated group | } |
| ? | special sequence | ? |

Based on these first elements from the EBNF, we can now define the elements of a gestural grammar, dedicated to 3D geometry, as follows:

sequence = gesture (operator gesture)* | relation'[gesture (operator gesture)*]';

gesture = contact (' characteristic (',' characteristic)*')' | characteristic (',' characteristic)*;

characteristic = element | element'('object')' | element'('contact_type')';

object = solid | axis | vertex | face | edge;

contact = [nb]'H' | [nb]'F' | [nb]'C';

H = hand;

F = finger;

C = generic contact;

contact_type = i | d;

d = direct;

i = indirect;

operator = '+' | ' * ' | ' , ' | '; ';

'+' = consecutive interactions;

'*' = simultaneous interactions;

',' = continuous interactions;

relation = PINCH | SPREAD | INTERSECTION;

element = identifier | shape;

identifier = HOLD | MOBILE | TAP;

shape = LINE | ARC['_'direction] | FREE;

reference = OR | SR | WR | CR;

OR = object reference;

SR = screen reference;

WR = world reference;

CR = camera reference;

direction = CW | ACW;

CW = clockwise;

ACW = anticlockwise;

location = SCREEN | SIDE | OUT;

OUT = out of the screen;

SIDE = border of the tactile surface;

SCREEN = tactile surface;

nb = [1-9][0-9]*;

### 3.3.3. *The prototype: FINGERS (Find INteractions for GEometry leaneRS)*

Our prototype is based on the taxonomy defined in the previous section for multi-touchscreens of reduced size, but as the state of the art showed, also for the other interactive possibilities of new technologies installed in the latest generations of tablets. In accordance with human-centered design, each choice was initially guided by educational, didactical and teaching reasons, thus justifying the choice of technology.

We aimed to evaluate any potential educational benefits of our prototype in the learning of 3D geometry for students aged between 9 and 15 years. The interactions we developed were, for the vast majority, tactile and based on multi-touch and so was named *FINGERS*© for **F**ind **IN**teractions for **GE**ometry learne**RS**. FINGERS manages all the tasks described by our gestural language and allows additional functions in order to adapt to the needs of both the students and teachers. We shall now describe the elements that guided our development of FINGERS.

### 3.3.3.1. *The menus (or rather their absence)*

From the start of our work, one main constraint played the important role of guiding thread in creating our prototype. In accordance with Decle's suggestions not to overload the screen by the addition of menus, we decided to bypass them entirely. One of our objectives was also to evaluate the speed of the assimilation of an interface made up solely of interactions. This avoids the interpretational difficulties of the iconography used in menus, a factor that is often aggravating for struggling students. This also allows us to avoid the use of a geometric vocabulary that could hinder certain students. Although learning the geometrical vocabulary is an explicitly stated aim of school curriculums, it can be useful to avoid it in certain research/investigation scenarios with students in order to allow them to more rapidly assimilate this type of activity. Furthermore, the particularity of this kind of manipulation with no menus showed during meetings with investors that the software was more appealing internationally.

### 3.3.3.2. *Implementation*

FINGERS was developed for Apple®'s iPads. It was installed and used on the iPad 2, new iPad and iPad Air. The iPad 2 is the minimal material version as it was the first to be equipped with a gyroscope. The implementation was carried out with objective-C and OpenGL ES 2.0 using the principles of object-oriented programming.

By basing the implementation on our taxonomy, the choice of technique was obvious. As the taxonomy is based on the selection of a solid, the number of contacts, their length, directivity and mobility, we implemented a state machine that was able to recognize the different modes. In this way, each new contact or action is analyzed and added to a dictionary of characteristics that is available at all times. As soon as one of the characteristics changes, the dictionary is updated and the state machine analyzes the newly obtained configuration.

### 3.3.4. *Our gestural language of interactions*

After having developed the grammar, we shall now look into expressing our resulting gestural language. During its development, we based our work on several principles, some of which are those of [KIN 11] (see section 2.4.2.1) to which we added the use of simple and single-handed movements for the four basic actions: creating an object, deleting it, translation (2 or 3 DoF) and rotation. For more specific actions such as duplication, assembly or managing nets, we allowed the use of two-handed gestures, as these make more sense for students relative to the task.

In this context, the objects manipulated are solids, particularly those studied in primary and middle school. These are classic polyhedrons such as cubes, cuboids, prisms and pyramids. Also part of this group are spheres, cones and cylinders. In the case of a polyhedron, teachers emphasized the importance of the availability of several possible representations, as it can be represented by:

– its faces;

– its edges (we included vertices in this representation);

– its faces, edges and vertices.

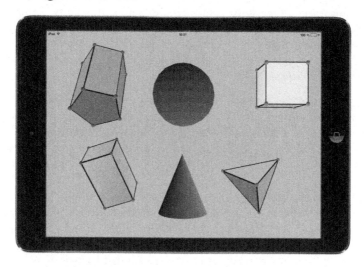

**Figure 3.7.** *Different solids in FINGERS*

3.3.4.1. *Selection/deselection*

The selection system based on our language is cyclical. It allows for different visualizations of one solid as well as additional interactions depending on the chosen visualization. The initial selection (state 1) makes the vertices and edges of the solid appear (Figure 3.8 (a)) which facilitates their counting and correctly delineates the faces.

A second selection makes the object's reference appear transparent (Figure 3.8 (b)). In this state (state 2), it is also possible to select one of the axes in order to carry out a rotation around it. The selected axis is no longer transparent in this case in order to give some visual feedback to the user (Figure 3.9 (a)). It is possible to go from the selection of one axis to another by directly selecting the new axis, with no need to pass through an intermediate deselection. Furthermore, the vertices are also selectable. The selection of two vertices defines a rotation axis that is represented by a green line (Figure 3.9 (b))

The third selection makes the object's reference disappear along with its faces (state 3), leaving only the edges and vertices (Figure 3.8 (c)). Finally, the fourth selection of the same solid brings it back to state 1.

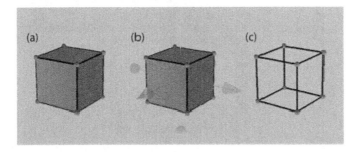

**Figure 3.8.** *Cyclical selection of a solid: a) state 1, solid represented with edges and vertices; b) state 2, solid as before with the object's reference; c) state 3, wire representation with only edges and vertices shown. For a color version of this figure, see www.iste.co.uk/bertolo/geometry.zip*

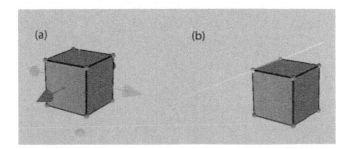

**Figure 3.9.** *Axis selection: a) state 2, solid with edges, vertices and reference shown, with one selected axis; b) definition of an axis of rotation by selection of two vertices. For a color version of this figure, see www.iste.co.uk/bertolo/geometry.zip*

To select a solid, direct contact held for 0.5 seconds is required (Figure 3.10(a)). In order to deselect it, an indirect and held contact of 0.5 seconds is required (Figure 3.10(c)). Initially we had designed the contacts to last 1 second but after several tests with users during our experiments, the feedback gathered from teachers and students was that this was too long. We thereby empirically determined that the most suitable length of time was a half-second.

In order to select an axis, a *TAP* is required on either the cone or sphere belonging to it (Figure 3.10(b)). To deselect it, another *TAP* is required on either its sphere or cone.

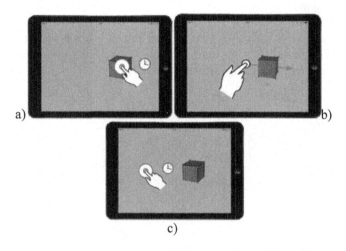

**Figure 3.10.** *Selection/deselection: a) selection of a solid; b) selection of an axis; c) deselection of a solid. For a color version of this figure, see www.iste.co.uk/bertolo/geometry.zip. (CC BY SA 2.0, Gestureworks. See http://gestureworks.com)*

In our grammar, this translates to the following:

SELECTION = 1F(HOLD(d, 0.5)) | 1F(TAP(d,axis));

DESELECTION = 1F(HOLD(i, 0.5));

### 3.3.4.2. *Translation*

We can distinguish between two types of translation. The first with 2 DoF in the plane of the screen and the second with 3 DoF. In both cases, these are carried out in the reference of the screen.

When a solid is not selected, a translation can be applied to it with 2 DoF by touching it with a finger and sliding it (Figure 3.11(a)). When the solid is selected, a translation with 2 DoF can be applied to it indirectly (or directly) by moving a finger along the screen (Figure 3.11(b)).

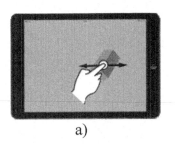

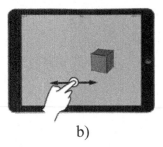

a)                                                  b)

**Figure 3.11.** *Translations with 2 DoF: a) direct translation; b) indirect translation. (CC BY SA 2.0, Gestureworks. See http://gestureworks.com)*

In the context of researching a movement that would be able to manage translations with 3 DoF, we explored three avenues: the Z-technique from [MAR 10a], the use of a spiral and finally, the one-handed, two-fingered movement that we ultimately chose.

Although the Z-technique is particularly interesting and relevant to a touchscreen tablet, as demonstrated by [MAR 10a], it was not chosen here for two reasons. The first was due to the size of the screen that makes a two-handed movement harder to carry out. The second reason, a consequence of the first, is linked to screen obscuring of the screen. In the use of a two-handed movement, a section of the screen is entirely occupied with depth management. We therefore chose a one-handed movement.

On the other hand, the principle of a spiral makes use of the screwing/unscrewing metaphor [VIV 12]. In this way, making a clockwise spiral, the direction of screwing moves the object along its Z-axis. An anti-clockwise spiral moves the object closer along its Z-axis (Figure 3.12).

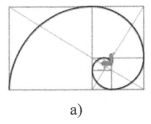

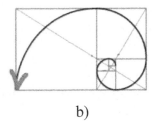

a)                                                  b)

**Figure 3.12.** *Principle of a spiral: a) screwing; b) unscrewing*

By coupling a spiral and a movement in the screen-plane, one obtains "a spring" that manages the translation of an object with 3 DoF (Figure 3.13).

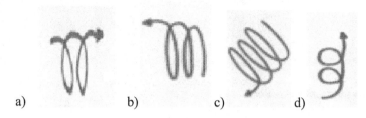

a)                     b)                     c)                     d)

**Figure 3.13.** *The spring: a) movement along X and –Z; b) movement along –X and Z, c) movement along 3 DoF, –X, –Y and –Z; d) movement along Y and Z*

Additional parameters can be used, such as the amplitude of the spirals, to determine the speed at which they move along the Z-axis. After having carried out several implementations that would allow the recognition of these spirals (Figure 3.14), this solution was not pursued further for the following reasons:

– the detection of this type of gesture is complicated. Although the ability to detect the number of spirals, their amplitude and direction is simple, the detection of the beginning of the movement remains problematic as is anticipating the moment the user decides to stop the movement. These problems lead to delays in the management of the movement and its application to the object, both of which can distract young users;

– this gesture leads to a lack of precision and requires real anticipation from the user when it comes to the object's trajectory, thus complicating the task at hand and increasing the cognitive effort of students rather than decreasing it.

This interaction is still under development in order to improve its use.

Therefore, to apply a transformation with 3 DoF, we kept in mind the use of the movement of two fingers on the screen in order to manage the translation across the screen as well as their movement apart from each other to control the depth of the object (Figure 3.15). If the two fingers move further away from each other, the solid comes closer and if the fingers move closer to each other, then the solid moves away. Depth movements can visually be translated as zooming. It seemed obvious to reuse this traditional movement in order to control the third dimension.

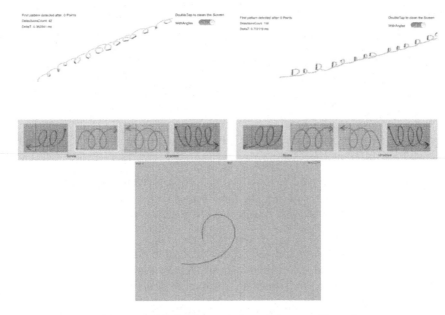

**Figure 3.14.** *Implementation and recognition of the spiral using two different techniques*

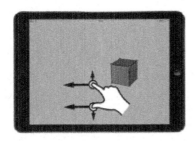

**Figure 3.15.** *Translation with 3 DoF: one-handed, two-fingered gesture. (CC BY SA 2.0, Gestureworks. See http://gestureworks.com)*

This is translated in our grammar by the following:

TRANSLATION = TRANSLATION_2DoF | TRANSLATION_3DoF;

TRANSLATION_2DoF = TRANSLATION_DIRECTE | TRANSLATION_INDIRECTE;

TRANSLATION_DIRECTE = 1F(MOBILE(d));

TRANSLATION_INDIRECTE = SELECTION + 1F(MOBILE(i));

TRANSLATION_3DoF = SELECTION + TRANSLATION_3D;

TRANSLATION_3D = 1F(MOBILE(i)) * 1F(MOBILE(i)) | 2F(MOBILE(i))*SPREAD

    | 2F(MOBILE(i))*PINCH

    | SPREAD(1F(MOBILE(i, LINE)) * 1F(MOBILE(i, LINE)))

    | PINCH(1F(MOBILE(i, LINE)) * 1F(MOBILE(i, LINE)));

### 3.3.4.3. *Rotation*

Three different types of rotation can be carried out using FINGERS, which take place in three different references:

1) free rotations FR with 3 DoF in a reference corresponding to that of the screen, of which the origin is located in the center of gravity of the object (Figure 3.16(a)). In this case, the axis of rotation is never explicitly defined, nor is it visible;

2) rotations with 1 DoF around each of the axes of the object's reference (OR) after the selection of the desired axis (Figure 3.16(c)). These rotations have the advantage of giving a higher positioning precision though the explicit definition of an axis;

3) rotations along an axis defined by two vertices of a solid (WR) and that are carried out in the world reference which is the mathematical scene reference (Figure 3.16(b)). It is then possible to pivot the solid as if it were being held between two fingers positioned at the vertices.

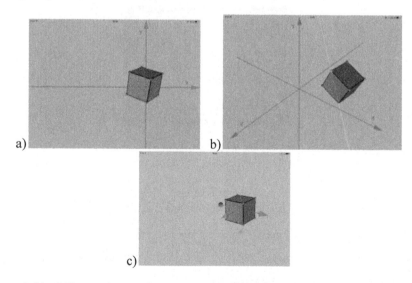

**Figure 3.16.** *Different types of rotations possible with FINGERS: a) rotation with 3 DoF in the reference of the screen; b) rotation in the reference around an axis defined by two vertices of the solid; c) rotation around an axis in the object's reference. For a color version of this figure, see www.iste.co.uk/bertolo/geometry.zip*

As the studies of [WOB 09], [HIN 11] and particularly those of [COH 12] have shown, the basic task that users struggle the most to suggest gestures for is rotation. [COH 12]'s study could not suggest an interaction that would better than another. During our first user experiments that will be described later in the book, we asked seven students aged between 9 and 15 years to tell us which movements they would use to rotate a cube around three axes on the screen reference. For rotations around the Z-axis, we obtained six propositions corresponding to the movement that is used by current tactile devices (Figure 3.17(a)). However, we also found six different propositions for rotations around the two other axes. We noted, as did [WOB 09], the pervasiveness of the WIMP paradigm, as we obtained suggestions such as those of the addition of a button or of sliders to control these two rotations.

In accordance with the principles of [KIN 11], who are proponents of the use of simple movements for frequent operations, as well as our principle of the use of one-handed gestures for this transformation, we have suggested the following interactions. To carry out a rotation around the Z-axis in the screen's reference, one must turn two fingers in the same direction (clockwise or anticlockwise) (Figure 3.17(a)). Based on rotations around the Z-axis that are carried out using two fingers, this characteristic was conserved for the other types of rotations. In order to apply a rotation around an axis which passes through the solid's center of gravity and is parallel to one of the two axes of the screen's reference, a translation must be applied using two fingers (Figure 3.17(b)). In the case of rotations around two axes of the screen plane, a horizontal displacement of the fingers leads to a rotation around the Y-axis, whereas a vertical one will lead to a rotation around the X-axis. Any other displacements lead to combinations of the two. Finally, in order to apply a rotation around either one of the axes of the object's reference or of an axis defined by two vertices of the solid, one must first select the axis and then move the fingers across the screen (Figure 3.17(c)).

a)                    b)                    c)

**Figure 3.17.** *Rotations: a) rotation around the Z-axis in the screen's reference; b) rotation around the red axes of the screen; c) rotation around an axis of the object's reference. For a color version of this figure, see www.iste.co.uk/bertolo/geometry.zip. (CC BY SA 2.0, Gestureworks. See http://gestureworks.com)*

In our grammar, this corresponds to the following:

ROTATION = SELECTION + ROTATION_SR | SELECTION + ROTATION_OR;

ROTATION_SR = 2F(MOBILE(i, LINE)) | 2F(MOBILE(i, ARC));

ROTATION_OR = SELECTION(axis) + 2F(MOBILE(i, LINE))

    | SELECTION(vertex1) + SELECTION(vertex2) +     2F(MOBILE(i, LINE));

### 3.3.4.4. *Exchange rotation–translation / translation–rotation*

As we have previously seen, the movements required for a translation with 3 DoF and for a rotation both use two fingers, potentially leading to ambiguity. In the implementation, our machine is tasked with removing these potential ambiguities. For example, if one carries out a translation during which a second finger touches the screen, the system will interpret this as the transition into a translation with 3 DoF. Indeed, there will then be 1*fm* + 1*fm*, rather than 2*fm* in the grammar and taxonomy. We have anticipated the case where the ambiguity remains and created a gesture that would allow one to change from a rotation to a translation with 3 DoF and *vice versa*. Alternatively, one can pass from the 3 DoF translation mode into the rotation mode by changing the state of the machine through a temporary interruption of one of the two contacts (Figure 3.18).

**Figure 3.18.** *Exchange between translation and rotation in the case of an un-eliminated ambiguity. (CC BY SA 2.0, Gestureworks. See http://gestureworks.com)*

In our grammar, this becomes the following:

EXCHANGE = 1F(HOLD(i)) * 1F(TAP(i));

### 3.3.4.5. *Nets*

In order to generate a net for a solid, it must be selected. We can then unfold or re-fold it using two fingers from each hand (indirect contacts) by moving them apart in opposite directions. Moving these two pairs of fingers away from each other manages the degree to which the net is opened. If the distance between the pairs of fingers increases then the pattern is opened up, and if it decreases then it closes (Figure 3.19(a)). It is also possible to separate all the faces of a solid in order to explore the creation of a net without the need for a predefined preposition. For this, one must move three contacts apart from each other (Figure 3.19(b)).

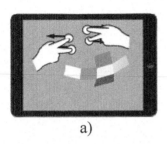
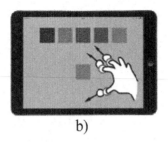

a)                                    b)

**Figure 3.19.** *Nets: a) opening; b) decomposition of the solid into its faces to recreate a net. For a color version of this figure, see www.iste.co.uk/bertolo/geometry.zip. (CC BY SA 2.0, Gestureworks. See http://gestureworks.com)*

This is translated into our grammar by the following:

OPENING = SPREAD(2H(2F(MOBILE(i, LINE)) * 2F(MOBILE(i, LINE))));

CLOSING = PINCH(2H(2F(MOBILE(i, LINE)) * 2F(MOBILE(i, LINE))));

MODIFICATION_NET = 1F(TAP(i)) + 1F(TAP(i));

SPLIT_FACE = SPREAD(2H(2F(MOBILE(i, LINE)) * 1F(MOBILE(i, LINE)))) | SPREAD(2F(MOBILE(i, LINE)) * 1F(MOBILE(i, LINE)));

Conforming to the needs and behaviors of teachers, once a solid has been developed and a net obtained from it, it can be manipulated in the same way as any other solid; but more importantly, it can also be modified. A double *TAP* on the screen positions it in the screen's plane (Figure 3.20(a)) and each face is then moveable in such a way as to be able to find the other possible net configurations of the solid (Figure 3.20(b)). To move the faces, there were several constraints, as follows:

– if a face cannot be topologically positioned in a convenient way, it automatically returns to its initial position;

– two faces can be linked only by an edge and not a vertex;

– when contact with the selected face is released, a magnetic effect will automatically place it onto the closest face with the ability of accommodating it.

Once the new net is finished, it needs to be closed again in order to confirm its validity. If it is correct, the solid is re-composed as before; if not the superimposed faces will be bicolored (Figure 3.20(c)). It is equally possible, as we have seen in the gestural language, to separate all the faces of a solid in order to re-constitute a potential net without using the initial base net suggested by the software. This newly obtained net can be moved as any other object.

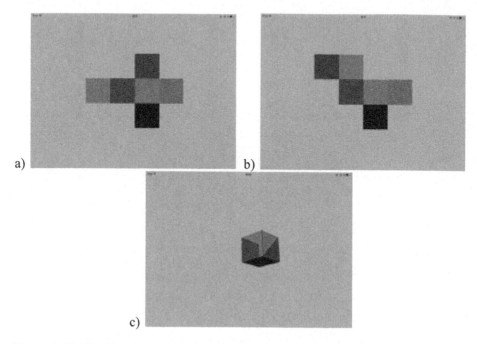

a)                                                      b)

c)

**Figure 3.20.** *Modification of the net of a solid: a) basic net generated by the software; b) net obtained through modification of the placement of the faces; c) verification of the validity of a net, with the bicolored face indicating two superimposed faces, indicating its invalidity. For a color version of this figure, see www.iste.co.uk/ bertolo/geometry.zip*

During the implementation of net-related functionalities, we met two main challenges:

– the first was verification of the constraints, in particular the one that meant that two faces had to be linked by an edge;

– the second was determination of the folding edges to close the net.

In order to overcome the first challenge, we put in place a verification system. In our structure, each face recognizes the other faces to which it is linked. In order to verify the validity of the structure obtained from the movement of a face, the system starts with the face that was moved. The structure is then studied, face by face, verifying that all of them have been processed. If one is missing, the structure obtained is not valid, otherwise it is. Figure 3.21 illustrates this solution. When face number 6 is moved, it is placed next to number 4. In the first iteration, the system begins at face 6, moving to number 4 (black arrow). The second iteration begins on number 4 and leads to numbers 2 and 5 (blue arrows). The dotted arrows indicate the paths that are not taken into account as they lead to previous faces. In the third iteration, face number 5 does not lead any further. Face number 2 leads to numbers 1 and 3. All of the faces of the cube were covered in this manner and therefore the structure is viable.

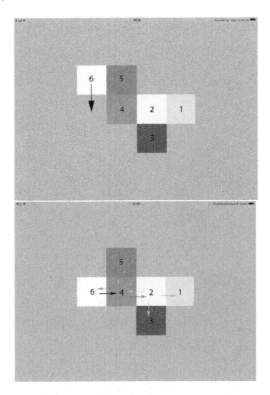

**Figure 3.21.** *Illustration of the validation algorithm after face movement. In this example, three iterations are needed to validate. The arrows of the same color indicated one same iteration. The dotted lines indicate paths that were not taken into account due to the fact that they lead to faces that were already taken into account. For a color version of this figure, see www.iste.co.uk/bertolo/geometry.zip*

In order to overcome the second challenge, determining the folding edges, we start with the face that has the most links, known as the main face. Each link is then considered as a folding axis. Using a recursive procedure, starting from the main face and leading to all of the ones it is linked to, we determine the folding edges between the faces, taking into account those over which we have already passed. The process stops once all the faces of the solid have been taken into account. Figure 3.22 illustrates this solution. In Figure 3.22(a) and (b), face 2 is the one with the most links to the other faces and is therefore considered the main face, with the three links becoming folding edges, represented in black in two cases. Faces 1 and 3 do not allow us to progress any further and so only face 4 remains. Figure 3.22(a) shows the passage from face 4 to 5, defining a folding edge (in white), followed by the passage between faces 5 and 6, defining in blue the last folding edge. The configuration of Figure 3.22(b) defines fewer steps, as access to the other faces takes place from face 4. The remaining folding edges are shown in blue.

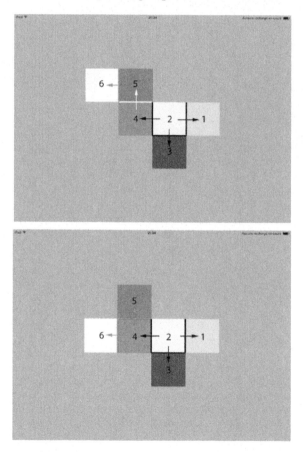

**Figure 3.22.** *Illustration of the folding edge determination algorithm.*
*For a color version of this figure, see www.iste.co.uk/bertolo/geometry.zip*

### 3.3.4.6. *Duplication*

As the duplication of a solid is a less frequent operation than others, it is managed via the use of a two-handed movement with three fingers. With the fingers of one hand, one finger points at the solid that is to be duplicated and holds onto it (direct contact). Then, with two fingers from the other hand, one "pulls" continuously (indirect contact) on the duplicated solid that emerges from the initial one (Figure 3.23(a)), or carries out a two-fingered *TAP* in the area where the supplicated solid is needed (Figure 3.23(b)).

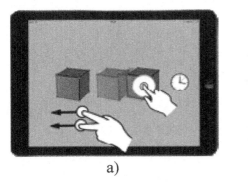

a)

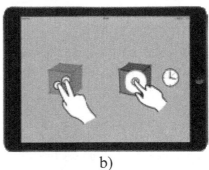

b)

**Figure 3.23.** *Solid duplication: a) continuous duplication;
b) duplication by teleportation. (CC BY SA 2.0,
Gestureworks. See http://gestureworks.com)*

This is translated in our grammar by the following:

DUPLICATION = 1F(HOLD(d)) * 2F(MOBILE(i)) | 1F(FIXE(d)) * 2F(TAP(i));

### 3.3.4.7. *Assembly*

The gesture defined for the assembly of two solids can be one- or two-handed depending on the distance separating the two solids. To carry out this operation, the two solids are translated directly towards each other (Figure 3.24). It is important to note that they can only be assembled if they have two identical faces, i.e. are superimposable. During the detection of contact on each solid, their orientation is automatically corrected so that two superimposable faces are in two parallel planes. As soon as two solids are close enough together, their juncture is automatic. If one of the contacts (or both) is stopped before juncture, both solids regain their initial orientation and position.

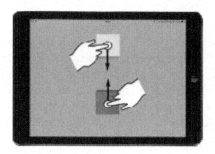

**Figure 3.24.** *Assembly of two solids. (CC BY SA 2.0,*
*Gestureworks. See http://gestureworks.com)*

This is translated in our grammar by the following:

ASSEMBLY = PINCH(1F(solid1, d) * 1F(solid2, d));

During the assembly of two solids, we made the choice to automatically correct the orientation of the solids in order to correctly align two identical faces which would link together. We were thereby confronted the challenge of aligning two solid's references in the orientation of a third reference. For this, we initially began with Euler's angles. Based on a vector product, we determined a normal vector to the zOZ plane that was used as a rotational vector in order to align the Z axes of each reference (Figure 3.25). Then, as the three references are orthonormal, all that is left is to align the orientation of the X and Y axes of each of the references through rotation around the Z-axis. In this way we were able to align the orientation of two references on that of a third reference through two rotations.

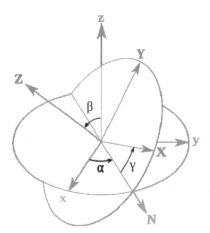

**Figure 3.25.** *The use of Euler's angles to align the orientation of two solids (source*
*Wikipedia). For a color version of this figure, see www.iste.co.uk/bertolo/geometry.zip*

### 3.3.4.8. *Management of the observer's point of view*

When we went into classrooms in order to observe students during their sessions working on 3D geometry, we were able to note the importance of manipulation and of models or physical solids, particularly in primary school children, although the tendency diminished up the years. In primary as well as the first two years of middle school, we saw that students stood and moved around to change their point of view in order to verify a result or to overcome a particular difficulty in their mental representation of the scene. Generally speaking, students would move around the scene. Having seen a teacher take pictures around the scene, the idea came to us to use the metaphor of the video camera, one already used by [TSA 02]. One simply needed to see the tablet as a window into the scene and by moving it in real life, one could change the observer's point of view of the scene (Figure 3.26).

To put this into place, we used the tablet's gyroscope to measure the angular speed along the three axes. This gave us the potential to manage 3 DoF. In order to activate the gyroscope, the tablet must be picked up with both hands and a finger set on each side of the tablet for a second (Figure 3.27). As soon as it is activated, the screen background changes color to give visual feedback to the user. The scene can thus be swiveled as if the user were sitting on a sphere. We also added the possibility of modifying the point at which the user aims their eye. For this, the screen must be *TAPPED* on one side and then any movement of the tablet no longer moves the observer but rather the direction they are looking in. In this way it is possible to pass from one mode to another. To leave observer management, the same gesture as was required to activate it is carried out again, that is two fingers on the side of the tablet for a second.

**Figure 3.26.** *Managing the observer around the scene as well as point of view using the gyroscope and metaphor of the video camera. For a color version of this figure, see www.iste.co.uk/bertolo/geometry.zip*

By integrating this interaction into FINGERS, we solved the problem of the placement of the observer during any change in point of view, a solution that we then evaluated.

**Figure 3.27.** *Gesture that activates the gyroscope*
*to change the point of view of the observer. (CC BY SA 2.0,*
*Gestureworks. See http://gestureworks.com)*

There remains one important challenge to overcome in order to render the software truly useable. All the interactions that we have put in place are there to manipulate solids, although at this point there is no interaction with the system that allows for the creation of solids or their introduction into the scene.

### 3.3.4.9. *Creation*

In accordance with our choice to not use menus, we instead used tangible artifacts in order to introduce solids into the scene (Figure 3.28(a)). From an educational, didactic and teaching point of view, this choice has a major advantage. One of the objectives of 3D geometry is to succeed in relating physical solids from real life with their planar representation. We have seen that the creation of mental representations in children is particularly difficult and that it is important to allow students to manipulate them in order to facilitate the creation of these representations. The use of tangible artifacts in the introduction of solids into the scene allows students to move real solids as well as transferring them in the program (Figure 3.28(b)). In this way, we hope that this will facilitate the association of these solids with their planar representation that will appear on the screen. The interactive side of such a program allows the manipulation of the virtual representation of the solid as well as the ability to work with it.

The creation of a solid in FINGERS therefore is very simple and requires a single interaction: putting the solid onto the screen makes it appear in the location it was placed.

From a technical point of view, the iPad screen is a capacitive screen. To ensure the recognition of the solid that will be dropped onto the screen, we used a base nearly entirely made up of conductive paint. It has six small feet made up of three larger ones and three smaller ones (Figure 3.28(a)). The smaller ones ensure stability of the base and are therefore not covered in this paint. The larger ones are painted and are contact points on the screen. The three contact points are set up following a particular configuration that ensures solid recognition. In Figure 3.28(a), these bases form an isosceles triangle, corresponding to the pattern of a cube in the recognition software.

It is important to note that in the two interactions already suggested by our gestural language, it is also possible to delete a solid using an eraser.

a)                                              b)

**Figure 3.28.** *Creation of a solid: a) contacts on a tangible solid taken into account through pattern detection; b) followed by the creation of the solid*

The creation of the solid uses three contacts of the multi-touch screen as well as tangible artifacts. This is translated as follows in our grammar:

CREATION = 3C(SCREEN);

### 3.3.4.10. *Deletion*

Just like creation, deletion can be carried out from a tangible artifact but we have also defined two movements that will lead to the deletion of a solid. The first is a direct translation, where the solid exits from any sides of the screen (Figure 3.29(a)). The second is the ability to use five fingers of the hand and bring them closer together, as though removing the object from the scene (Figure 3.29(b)). Even though this movement remains, it was not chosen for use with students in the development of the prototype as it was revealed to be too complex, requiring several attempts to delete the object, whereas the first one had a 100% success rate at the first try.

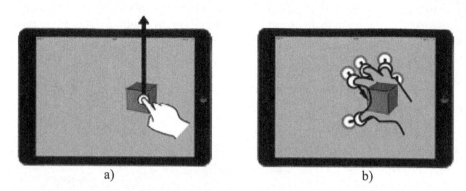

**Figure 3.29.** *Deletion of a solid: a) by removing it from the screen; b) by picking it up. (CC BY SA 2.0, Gestureworks. See http://gestureworks.com)*

This is translated in our grammar by the following:

DELETION = SELECTION + TRANSLATION_DIRECTE(OUT)

| SELECTION + PINCH(5F(MOBILE(i, LINE)));

During implementation of the movement involving five fingers of one hand, we came up against the difficulty of recognition of this movement. From a physiological point of view, the use of all the fingers from one hand is difficult and moving them all closer together usually leads to loss of at least one contact. To overcome this challenge, we took into account the number of contacts at the start of the interaction, followed by moving together three of these contacts, allowing the loss of two of these without leading the movement to failure. Despite this solution being put into place, the movement was not recognized with a sufficiently high success rate for it to be used by students.

We now have a prototype named FINGERS that takes into account not only the language of interactions but also part of the technological elements of the tablet. Although we explored a few different paths in the use of the camera (in color recovery for example), they were not taken forward or needed further development before they become useful alternatives.

## 3.4. Evaluation of the acceptance of interactions (selection, translation and rotation)

Until now, we have discussed the material choices that were made, followed by the implementation of interactions with the aim of allowing us to overcome our double challenge:

– usability;

– educational benefit in the teaching of 3D geometry through the decreasing the cognitive load, induced by the use of tactile associated with our interactions.

In this section, we shall describe the experiments linked to the acceptance and usability of our modes of interaction. The educational section will be described in the following chapter. Our evaluations can be separated into two categories:

– the acceptance and usability of the interactions linked to rotation and the observer's changing point of view;

– the ease of learning and memorizing the interactions.

These experiments are not presented here in chronological order but Figure 3.30 places them in the global experimental context.

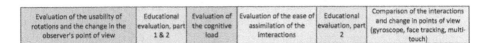

| Evaluation of the usability of rotations and the change in the observer's point of view | Educational evaluation, part 1 & 2 | Evaluation of the cognitive load | Evaluation of the ease of assimilation of the Imteractions | Educational evaluation, part 2 | Comparison of the interactions and change in points of view (gyroscope, face tracking, multi-touch) |
|---|---|---|---|---|---|

**Figure 3.30.** *Plan of experiments in the acceptability and usability of the interactions*

### 3.4.1. *Experimental challenges and constraints*

One of the main difficulties of experiments carried out in the classroom is the access to children. Indeed, carrying out experiments with children aged between 9 and 15 years (and therefore minors) requires the permission of the educational system, passing through the academic inspection, the head of the establishment, and finally the classroom teacher. Also required is agreement from the parents. Although the educational system is generally favorable towards these experiments, this is always very time-consuming. Furthermore, one must find teachers willing to open the door to their classroom as well as generally being favorable towards the use of new technologies in teaching. This also requires of them a certain time investment in terms of consultation in order to prepare and plan these interventions during the course of these experiments. These teachers are not rare but it is important to note the difficulties associated with carrying out experiments with young students in order to understand the process of evaluation. If problems are encountered during one of these experiments, the class work must stop in order to prevent any bias in the study.

### 3.4.2. *Preliminary evaluation of the acceptance of rotation and point of view change interactions*

After having developed the prototype, it was improved bit by bit through our experiments. Logically, the first interactions were basic ones, used for selecting, carrying out translations and rotations, but also for changing the point of view of the user in order to better visualize the scene. So our first evaluation related to the usability and acceptance of rotation and point of view-changing interactions for the user [BER 13a].

#### 3.4.2.1. *Participants*

Our first study was made up of seven participants. All were students from the third cycle, aged between 10 and 15 years (average age, 11.6 years, standard deviation, 1.59). None of the students were color-blind. In order to choose a group of representative students from an average class, we sought in this small group to find three different potential habitual-users of tablets. Two of the students had never used a tactile tablet or smartphone, four of them were already habitual users and one had his own tablet.

#### 3.4.2.2. *Material*

Each participant had their own iPad equipped with FINGERS software as well as a response sheet for each of the tests carried out. During this experiment, FINGERS carried out translations in the plane of the screen as well as all rotations and changes in the observer's point of view. The creation of solids was not yet implemented at this stage and therefore two other types of software were also installed. The first was a training program where the scene was made up of blue cubes, one of which had a single hidden red face. The second was equivalent to the tests made up of a scene of five cubes, of which some had a hidden red face, the number of which varied between one and four. The number of cubes was chosen in order not to favor the individual rotation of the cubes or the change of the observer's point of view.

### 3.4.2.3. *Task*

The experiment was carried out over three days. During the first, we asked each participant to answer two questions:

1) What movements would you carry out to turn the cube in this way?

2) What movements would you make to "see" any face of the cube without touching it?

For each of these questions we used a physical cube in order to explain the rotations in question, and the participant would show their response on a tablet with a cube in the scene.

Following this, during each of the seven tests carried out over the two sessions, the participants were asked to find both the number of cubes with a red face and the initial position of each of the red faces that were found (Figure 3.31).

 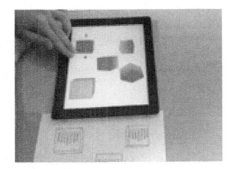

**Figure 3.31.** *Task no. 2: finding cubes with a red face and their position*

### 3.4.2.4. *Experimental plan*

The experiments were split into four phases as follows:

– *Phase 1*: We verified the competencies of each participant in the use of a touchscreen tablet in order to verify the validity of our sample. For this, the participants were required to reproduce a summary construction in Lego© using the *Blocks*! software which allows the manipulation of Lego pieces. We then asked each participant to carry out the first task.

– *Phase 2*: The following day, we presented the software to each participant for three minutes and gave them the second task to carry out. They were then able to practice using the interactions with the software designed to this effect for five minutes. This moment was also used to verify that each participant had understood the task. A session of three tests was then carried out.

– *Phase 3*: The second session took place a week later with four tests this time. No reminder was given regarding the interactions at play but students were allowed to ask for one if needed.

– *Phase 4*: The participants were asked to complete a questionnaire to give their opinion on the ease of use and intuitiveness of the interactions based on the Likert scale on eight points. We then interviewed each participant in order to gather their feelings and additional information.

During each of the tests over the two sessions, we timed the participants and filmed the tablet and their hands. The interactions used by the students were recorded.

### 3.4.2.5. *Results and discussion*

As we have already stated during the description of rotational movements, the answers to the first question of task 1 were all different and imbibed with the WIMP paradigm. The answers regarding the rotations around two axes of the plane are as follows:

– the use of buttons;

– the use of sliders (twice);

– the use of a vertex to guide the rotation;

– a gesture consisting of moving a finger perpendicularly to an edge;

– a two-handed movement with a finger to fix a vertex or an edge in order to pivot the cube;

– the use of a horizontal or vertical indirect finger movement.

These answers therefore confirmed the studies of [WOB 09] and [COH 11].

The second question regarding the change in the observer's point of view only yielded three answers:

– using fingers indirectly in order to pivot the whole scene (twice);

– to lean to the side, above or below in order to be able to see the hidden faces (three times);

– taking the tablet in the user's hands and using it to swivel around the scene (twice).

It is interesting to note that for the latter two propositions, students hesitated in their answer and most of the time started with "I know that is not possible but...". The first solution can be interpreted as a complete rotation of the scene rather than a change in the point of view, and is therefore not desirable from an educational point of view. The second solution can be carried out using the camera and is interesting but leads to difficulties in "seeing" the back faces. The last one is the one that we had chosen.

Figure 3.32 shows the average time needed to carry out each test. During the first one carried out by the participants, the average time was 198.7 s (standard deviation = 121.9). We should note that the standard deviation is large here, and is explained by the make-up of our sample. The student who had never used a tactile terminal took 6 m 42 s to carry out the task. The average time decreased from task to task, to reach 69.1 s (standard deviation = 28.4 s). We can note two interesting elements. Firstly that the time required to carry out the task at the end of the seven tests was divided by three. Secondly, that the standard deviation also decreased strongly, indicating that all the students improved the time they required, and that all the times were close, whether or not the students were in the habit of using this type of device. Finally, there is a noticeably small increase in the time required for the first test of the second session (test 4). This increase is due to the week between the two sessions. At this point, several students searched for interactions used to manipulate the cubes. However, none of the participants asked for the reminder they were allowed, and consequently they were all able to remember the interactions after one week.

Figure 3.33 shows the percentage of successful attempts at each task for all the participants. We can easily see that from the second test, students systematically found the exact number of cubes with a red face. However, although the success rate was high, at no point did they manage to find all the initial positions. Again, we note small regression at the fourth test, which is explained once more by the week's break between the two sessions, confirmed by the participants during their final interviews.

The rapid decrease in the time required for each task for all participants, added to their high success rate as well as the fact that none of them asked for a reminder in order to remember the interactions, indicate that our chosen interactions for managing rotations and changes in the observer's point of view were accepted as well as assimilated by the participants.

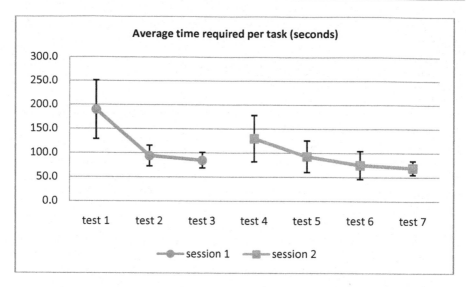

**Figure 3.32.** *Average and standard deviation of the time (in sec.) required by the participants to carry out the task*

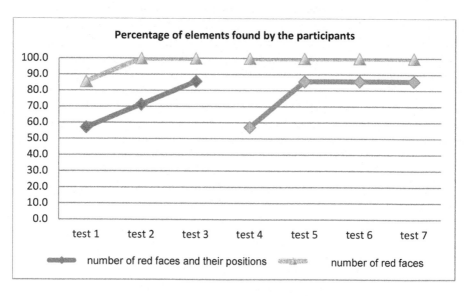

**Figure 3.33.** *Percentage of successful attempts at the "finding the red faces" task for all participants*

The user feedback suggests that our chosen interactions were positively received. Indeed, the gestures were easy to use (Figure 3.34(a)) and intuitive (Figure 3.34(b)), although two of them were found to be largely favored by the users. Discussions with the participants suggest that the rotations around axes of the solid's reference (OR) using both multi-touch and changes in the observer's point of view (CPV) by swiveling around the scene using the gyroscope were seen as more efficient. The main reasons put forward by the students were the fact that selecting a rotation axis prevents parasitic object movements as well as the fact that swiveling around the scene is the most intuitive and "natural" interaction. Our recordings of the interactions used during the tests (Figure 3.34(c)) confirm that the two interactions put forward were the most frequently used. We may also note that by using the OR rotation, five selections are required along with ten rotations in order to be sure to observe all the faces, whereas all that is required is to swivel around the scene and look over and under it using the changing point of view in order to carry out the task. Furthermore, we were able to observe that two of the participants were using OR in order to verify their CPV obtained results.

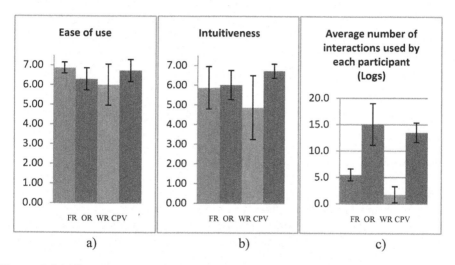

**Figure 3.34.** *Feedback on the interactions by users (FR: rotation with 3 DoF, OR: rotation around an axis of the object's reference, WR: rotation around an axis defined by two vertices, CPV: change in the point of view using the gyroscope): a) ease of use; b) intuitiveness; c) register of interactions*

Rotations with 3 DoF (FR) were used very little even though they allowed the user to carry out the task more rapidly than through the use of OR, as there is no need to select the rotation axis each time. The participants remarked that locking an axis seemed useful to them, essentially in order to avoid parasitic and unwanted rotations. Video recordings showed that students had some difficulties carrying out purely vertical or horizontal movements. In the case of FR, they did not consider themselves fully able to manage the rotations of the cube. Only one participant used FRs for all the tests. Three only used rotations around axes defined by two vertices (WR) but only one truly used it to carry out the task. The definition of a rotation axis of this kind is not necessary in order to complete the task and the number of additional interactions required may explain the low use of this movement. Although the experience was designed in order to evaluate rotations, we were able to observe one of the participants try to initially answer the questions by using translations, moving the cube to the left-hand side of the screen in order to observe the right face and so on. Finally, students remarked that the "coolest" interaction was the use of the gyroscope in changing points of view and navigating the scene.

This evaluation allowed us to see students employing strategies that made use of different complementary interactions such as rotation around an object's axis and the change in point of view using the gyroscope; thus showing that multi-touch and sensors complete each other. Furthermore, discussions with the users confirmed this acceptance of the interactions. But they also showed that for participants, the selection of an axis implies applying a rotation to an object. In this case, they do not see the point of using both fingers intended for the gesture by our language and would rather only use one. Due to the small sample size, it was necessary to carry out other experiments before eventually integrating this observation.

### 3.4.3. *Comparison between gyroscope, face-tracking and multi-touch*

As we have stated several times, one of the elements that led us to choose a tablet-type mobile device is the potential to move it in order to change a point of view through the user's physical movement. During our first experiment, we received three suggestions from seven students for managing the change in point of view. The interesting parts of these three suggestions is that they rely on three different technologies that are available on tablets: multi-touch, camera and gyroscope. We shall now compare them in order to determine which would be the best accepted and most easily used by students.

#### 3.4.3.1. *Participants*

To carry out this experiment we used a class of Year 6 (average age 11 years) students in a school in Metz (France). The class was made up of 30 students but only 28 were present for this evaluation. None of the students were color blind. It is also important to note that only one of them had never used a mobile device previously. Of the 27 remaining students, 16 had their own smartphone or tablet.

### 3.4.3.2. *Material*

An iPad was given to each of the participants. It was equipped with training software and five test programs for each technology (multi-touch, camera, gyroscope), or a total of 18 programs. For each one, the initiation of the change in point of view interaction was identical and corresponded to a contact on either side of the tablet with a thumb for one second. The passage into the change of point of view mode was signaled by a color change at the back of the screen, to provide visual feedback to students. For multi-touch, the use of two fingers allowed the change of point of view following 3 DoF (as with the applying rotations in our gestural language). With the gyroscope, we had taken the previously developed part of FINGERS. Finally, for the camera we used the face-tracking technology developed by the IIHM team from Joseph Fourier University of Grenoble for i3D.

Each test program was made up of three colored cubes, one of which had a red face, another two red faces and the last one none (Figure 3.35(a)). Each test program was made up of five differently colored cubes with between one and three red faces. In each of the programs, there were between one and four cubes that only had a single red face (Figure 3.35(b)).

**Figure 3.35.** *Experimental programs: a) training program; b) test program*

For each series of tests associated with a given technology, the students were given an answer sheet. For each test, five tickboxes representing the five colors were available.

### 3.4.3.3. Task

During the experiments, students were required to find all the cubes that had only a single red face and then tick the correctly colored box on their sheet.

### 3.4.3.4. Experimental plan

The experiment was made up of the four following phases:

– *Phase 1*: A questionnaire that aimed to find out whether the student had already used tactile smartphones or tablets was distributed and completed. It was then used in the creation of homogeneous groups in terms of use and possession of touchscreen devices.

– *Phase 2*: One week later, four groups of five students and two of four were established. The handover took place within the school, in a specially designated room on the same level as the student's classroom. Two researchers were present to watch the students, give tasks and take notes of their observations as well as timing the tasks. The six sessions were planned over a whole day but in the end were carried out over a day and a half. This was due to breaks and having to move down the corridors, with each session lasting an hour, including moving between classrooms and answering the questionnaires.

Each session was split in the following way:

1) collecting the group of students from their classroom and taking them to the room the experiments were held in;

2) explanation of the experiments and instructions linked to the task;

3) presentation of the first technology, followed by 2 minutes of training on the dedicated program;

4) the five timed tests being carried out;

5) presentation of the second technology, followed by a 2-minute training period;

6) the five timed tests take place;

7) presentation of the third technology, followed by a 2-minute training period;

8) the five timed tests take place.

The technologies were counterbalanced throughout the groups as follows:

| Group | Face-tracking | Gyroscope | Multi-touch |
|---|---|---|---|
| 1 | 1 | 2 | 3 |
| 2 | 1 | 3 | 2 |
| 3 | 2 | 1 | 3 |
| 4 | 3 | 1 | 2 |
| 5 | 2 | 3 | 1 |
| 6 | 3 | 2 | 1 |

– *Phase 3*: In each group, the students filled out a post-test questionnaire asking them to rank the interactions in order of preference. They then gave their opinion on the difficulty, the fun and intuitiveness of each technique. Each opinion was gathered on a scale of four choices (very difficult/difficult/easy/very easy). Finally, they were able to suggest an improvement and/or a new interaction that would be used to manage the change in point of view.

– *Phase 4*: Debriefing with the whole class.

In order to carry out a classification of the interactions by preference, two criteria were specified:

– the number of students who ordered a given interaction in first place;

– the score obtained by weighting the rankings: 1 point for first place, 0.5 points for second and 0 for third.

The same was done for the verification of results of the cube tests with a single red face. We attributed one point per red cube found and -1 for every error. Forgetting a cube did not lead to any loss of marks. In each series, there were ten cubes with a single red face to be found over the five tests.

To summarize: 28 students x 3 technologies x 5 tests: 420 changes of points of view.

### 3.4.3.5. *Results and discussion*

Figure 3.36 shows the median number of cubes that have a single red face that were found by students depending on the type of interaction used. The results are very close for the three techniques with eight cubes for multi-touch and seven cubes for the gyroscope and face-tracking. ANOVA ($F_{2.81} = 0.669$; $p = 0.515$) analysis did not show any significant differences. We can consider the three to be effective.

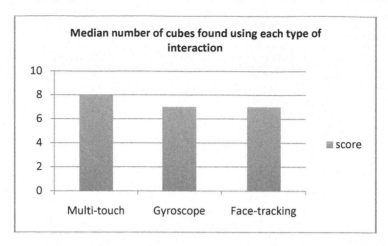

**Figure 3.36.** *Median number of cubes with a single red face found by the students depending on the type of interaction used*

The students were timed when carrying out the tasks and the average time required to complete the task using the multi-touch was 41.2 s; with the gyroscope, it was 45.8 s and with face-tracking, 108.6 s. We can see that the average times are close for both multi-touch and the gyroscope. Face-tracking required approximately 2.5x more time for students to complete the task. Figure 3.37 shows the average time required to carry out the task depending on the type of interaction used. We can see that for multi-touch and the gyroscope the average time required for each test does not vary much and remains nearly constant. However, for face-tracking there is a notable decrease in the average time required to carry out the tests during the sessions. As we described, the group of students were already smartphone and tablet users. They were therefore in the habit of using multi-touch and sensors such as the accelerometer, as 25 of the 28 participants admitted to using their device for gaming among other things. Furthermore, as the students were allowed to stand up and move around in order to use the different technologies, they did not hesitate in doing so in order to use the gyroscope (Figure 3.38(a)). In the case of camera use for face-tracking, this interaction is new and requires learning. The average time required per test decreases with their use. Another essential point in the understanding of this difference is the sensibility of this technique to lighting conditions. We spent a certain amount of time partially opening and closing the blinds in order to conserve optimum lighting conditions for use. We had not planned a calibration system for the position of the face as in the case of i3D. Students used their reflection in the screen to position themselves correctly. One last point that may also explain these differences is that of the children's motility. We also observed that even when students were able to position themselves correctly and rapidly, they lost the face-tracking rapidly if movements were of too high an amplitude as was generally the case. Figure 3.38(b) shows the face-tracking method of use. We were able to observe a strategy that fits with a motility problem in children. In group 3, the group with the lowest average time required per use of this technique, one of the students set the tablet on his chair before leaning over it over the back of his chair. He was constrained in his movements and as such managed to use the face-tracking without any problem. After a few moments, the other students in the group imitated him. During the final debriefing, the participants suggested the addition of a small window that would provide visual feedback as to the position of the face during use, enabling them to adjust their movements and the position of the tablet.

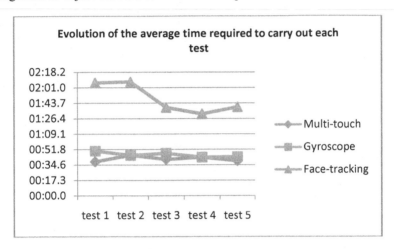

**Figure 3.37.** *Evolution of the average time (in minutes and seconds) taken to carry out each test*

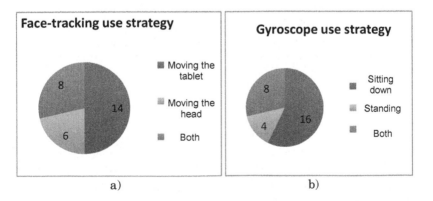

**Figure 3.38.** *Student's strategies for using interactions: a) face-tracking; b) gyroscope*

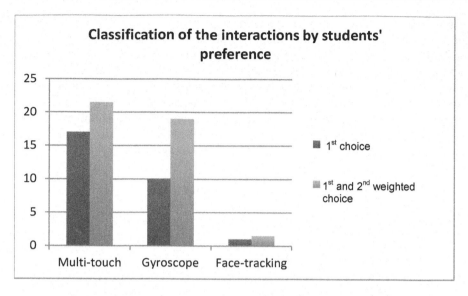

**Figure 3.39.** *Classification of the interactions carried out by the students. In dark gray: the number of students who ranked an interaction in first place. In light gray: the weighted score obtained by taking into account the interactions that were ranked second by students*

In their answers to the questionnaires, the students overwhelmingly supported the multi-touch, followed by the gyroscope and then the camera with face-tracking (Figure 3.39). Participants found the multi-touch to be very easy to use, the gyroscope easy and the face-tracking technology difficult for the aforementioned reasons. In the answers to the questionnaires, 21 students expressed the loss of face acquisition as being the main difficulty, expressing it in different ways: "it loses your face", "there's a bug", "it gets stuck", "it can't find my face". In the case of the gyroscope, students did not always want to be able to manage 3 DoF and the debriefing showed that they would rather have been able to block the changes in point of view around the Z-axis, which they found not to be useful and which generated parasitic movements. Regarding the multi-touch, they would have preferred an interaction that only required the use of one finger. Participants did however find the use of the multi-touch to be a lot of fun, the gyroscope and the face-tracking both fun. Finally, they found the multi-touch to be very intuitive whereas the gyroscope and face-tracking were both simply intuitive. We must admit at this point that we did not expect these results, particularly not such enthusiasm towards multi-touch, as from our point of view it was definitely the less intuitive of the three techniques. During the debriefing, we asked the children about this point. They explained their choice by saying it was technology that they used on a daily basis on their phones or tablets, that they have at home and consequently what they consider to be more "normal" to use or "the first thing they think of". Whereas [WOB 09] referred to the pervasiveness of the WIMP paradigm, for new generations who are equipped from an early age with touchscreen devices (25 students have one at home and 16 have their own) the new paradigm is that of the tactile multi-touch, and, as in the case of [WOB 09]'s study, the participants are attached to their paradigm.

As we have already seen in our state of the art, from an educational point of view it is not recommended for the multi-touch to be used in changes in points of view. Furthermore, this study confirms our choice of gyroscope use, which has proven to be easier to use as well as more robust, as it does not depend on light conditions, for example. However, the students did suggest modifications that may be useful, such as the removal of 1 DoF. It would be interesting to repeat a comparative study, taking into account the students' comments and including a small window that would allow students to receive constant visual feedback which may mitigate some of the breaks in tracking. This is even more interesting when one considers that four students suggested a new or improved interaction: the use of eye-tracking!

### 3.4.4. *Student learning of prototype interactions*

After having evaluated several interactions in our program, and before beginning the next chapter regarding the evaluation of the educational benefits of software such as FINGERS in a teaching context, we developed an experiment to measure the ease or lack of learning these interactions. The easier these are to assimilate, the higher the chances that they decrease students' cognitive load as well as allowing them to concentrate not on the use of the software but on the task at hand as well as the concept at play.

#### 3.4.4.1. *Participants*

During this experiment, we used a class of Year 7s (average age 12 years) in a middle school located in Pont-à-Mousson (France). This class was made up of 22 students, and of them 20 participated in the experiment until the end. All students had already used a device such as a smartphone or touchscreen tablet and 17 of them already had their own device. According to both the school and their mathematics teacher, the class was regarded as difficult and with a strong tendency towards distraction. The students were split into two homogeneous groups based on their answers to a questionnaire and with the help of their teacher.

### 3.4.4.2. *Material*

One iPad was given out to every pair of students. FINGERS was installed on each iPad with two different versions: the first where most of the interactions were hidden in order to stop the students from accessing them before the right time; and the second, the complete version where all interactions were available. During each session, the students were given exercise sheets with their corresponding answer sheets. A neighboring classroom was provided to us for the duration of the experiment, allowing us to separate the two groups.

### 3.4.4.3. *Task*

Each student from one of the groups (student 1) assimilated some of the interactions and then used them in solving an exercise. The student then was required to explain these interactions to a student from the other group (student 2), with whom he or she formed a pair. Then, student 2 solved an identical exercise using a tablet, with the aid of the newly learned interactions. The idea at play here is that should the explanations of the task allow the second student to carry it out correctly, these would be considered as simple to explain and easy to assimilate (learning via a third party).

### 3.4.4.4. *Experimental plan*

The experiments were carried out over three weeks, taking place every Thursday during a mathematics period. The experimental plan was as follows: during the first two weeks, the group that received the explanation of FINGERS use was in a different room so that they second group could not overhear them. During the emitting/receiving situation, a student from group 1 was paired with one from group 2. The experimental periods were carried out in an hour of class, which realistically only came down to 50 minutes, so the two sessions (learning followed by restitution to a classmate) were only each 25 min long.

Session 1:

– *Group 1:*

- discovering the program and explanation of the interactions for 10 min (selection, translation and rotation);

- carrying out the mathematics exercise using FINGERS and immediate evaluation of the success rate;

- return to the classroom;

- explanation of the useful interactions to a student from group 2 in order to allow them to complete the exercise.

*– Group 2:*

- no previous explanation or discovery of FINGERS;

- pairing with a student from group 1;

- watching the student from group 1 giving explanations regarding the exercise and use of FINGERS to solve it;

- carrying out an identical exercise to group 1 using FINGERS.

Session 2:

- evaluation of both groups on the interactions previously seen.

*– Group 2:*

- discovering the program and explanation of the interactions during 10 min (pattern generation and modification);

- carrying out the mathematics exercise using FINGERS and immediate evaluation of the success rate;

- return to the classroom;

- explanation of the useful interactions to a student from group 1 in order to allow them to complete the exercise.

*– Group 1:*

- no previous explanation or discovery of FINGERS;

- pairing with a student from group 2;

- watching the student from group 2 giving explanations regarding the exercise and use of FINGERS to solve it;

- carrying out an identical exercise to group 2 using FINGERS.

Session 3:

– evaluation of both groups regarding the interactions of the previous week.

We observed the handover of the task to the students in order to manage the validity of the information given, but it must be noted that we did not intervene at any point during the transmission of information in pairs. Table 3.3 summarizes the protocol put into place during the sessions.

| Week | Group 1 | Group 2 |
|---|---|---|
| | Diagnostic tests and group formation | |
| 1 | Discovery of the program (selection, translation and rotation)<br><br>Verification of the understanding of the interactions<br><br>Completion of an exercise<br><br>Evaluation of the success of the exercise and interactions used.<br><br>Explanation of the useful interactions to group 2 | Carrying out an identical exercise to group 1 using FINGERS and the explanations of group 1 regarding the interactions (Verification of the quality of the information transmitted by the students) |
| | Evaluation of the retained interactions (selection, translation and rotation) | |
| 2 | Carrying out an identical exercise to group 2 using FINGERS and the explanations of group 2 regarding the interactions (Verification of the quality of the information transmitted by the students) | Discovery of the program (net manipulation / modification)<br><br>Verification of the understanding of the interactions<br><br>Completion of an exercise<br><br>Evaluation of the success of the exercise and interactions used.<br><br>Explanation of the useful interactions to group 1 |
| 3 | Evaluation of the retained interactions (net manipulation) | |

**Table 3.3.** *Test protocol for the Year 7s*

### 3.4.4.5. *Results and discussion*

As the objective here was not to monitor the progress in the learning of 3D geometry, but rather the learning of interactions, we will not describe the exercises that the students were asked to do, which were only a pretext for the experiments. During the presentation of the results, we considered a movement to be learned from the moment a student was able to use it without hesitation or repeated attempts to find it. Otherwise it was considered not to have been learned. Figure 3.40 shows the comparison between percentages of acquisition of different interactions at the end of their first learning session and at the end of the experiment after three weeks. We noted that students overwhelmingly learned the basic interactions, such as selection and translation, as this was the case for all but one of the students at the end of the first session. Rotations were also required in the manipulation of nets and so we could measure their progress without needing to go over their learning again. The opening and closing as well as face separation interactions were not learned as effectively after a week's use of the program. These two interactions are only used in specific cases of working on nets and will therefore require more in-depth learning than the basic interactions did. We can still conclude that the interactions that were presented to the students are easily assimilated, and after a 10-min presentation to each group the students were able to transmit these skills to their classmates. Five out of the seven interactions we presented had an assimilation rate of 90% or more and only one of them reached only 55%, where the interaction was linked to a specific and infrequent action.

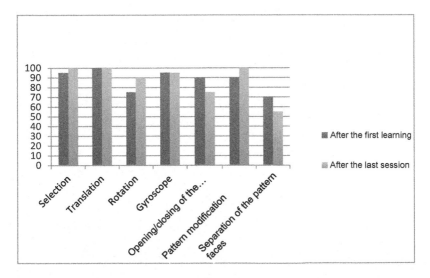

**Figure 3.40.** *Comparison of acquisition of the different interactions (FINGERS) by students between the first learning and the last sessions as percentages*

## 3.5. Conclusion and perspectives

In this chapter, we presented our user-centered approach and showed the benefits of taking into account users' needs and habits. We carried out a comparative study of pre-existing software functionalities and highlighted where they were lacking. Based on the principles put forward in our state of the art as well as educational principles, we then formalized both a gestural language and grammar that aimed to overcome these deficiencies. Consequently, we hope to make these accessible to students aged between 9 and 15 years, and as a result decrease their cognitive load, allowing them to concentrate on solving the task at hand and learning 3D geometry rather than the use of software and its interface. In the first evaluations we presented, we validated some of our choices and showed that our software showcased these interactions. FINGERS, was rapidly assimilated by students. Table 3.4 summarizes the technology required by each interaction in the use of the software in a 3D geometry learning context.

| Interactions | Interaction technology | | |
|---|---|---|---|
| | multi-touch | sensors | tangible |
| Selection / deselection | ✓ | ✗ | ✗ |
| Translation | ✓ | ✗ | ✗ |
| Rotation | ✓ | ✗ | ✗ |
| Exchange rotation–translation | ✓ | ✗ | ✗ |
| Change in point of view | ✗ | ✓ | ✗ |
| Net | ✓ | ✗ | ✗ |
| Duplication | ✓ | ✗ | ✗ |
| Assembly | ✓ | ✗ | ✗ |
| Creation | ✗ | ✗ | ✓ |
| Suppression | ✓ | ✗ | ✓ |

**Table 3.4.** *Summary of the technology required by each interaction in the context of learning 3D geometry*

From Table 3.4 we can extrapolate the links between three main categories that are associated with three types of technology used. The creation/suppression interactions are linked to tangible interfaces, manipulation interactions to multi-touch and the navigation/change of point of view interactions to sensors. Table 3.5 shows our first classification of interactions based on the entry system used.

| Interactions | Entry system | | |
|---|---|---|---|
| | *multi-touch tactile surface* | *sensor* | *tangible* |
| Creation/suppression | ◔ | ✕ | ◔ |
| Manipulation | ◔ | ✕ | ✕ |
| Navigation/change in point of view | ✕ | ◔ | ✕ |

**Table 3.5.** *Classification of interactions based on their entry system*

In the following chapter, we will evaluate the educational benefits of our interactions through the use of FINGERS in real classroom situations. It is important to note that the work that was already carried out leads to a continuation of taking the users' needs into account and through this including functionalities and interactions that would meet a certain number of needs, some of which were not met and some that were being developed, such as color management or the potential of select several objects in order to apply the same transformation to them all. But there are two main points that have still not been covered. The first, the dynamic scaling of solids, characterizing the term *dynamic* geometry. During any modifications made to a solid, its mathematical properties must be conserved. A cube can therefore not be extruded in order to form a cuboid, for instance, and this is what differentiates educational from modeling software. The second point relates to the portioning of solids using a plane, of which middle school teachers and students have a particular interest, particularly Year 10s. These two points will be the work of future projects based on the developments using FINGERS.

# Evaluation of the Educational Benefits for 3D Geometry

More and more schools are equipping themselves with tablets in the hope that they will lead to educational benefits. Both principals and teachers are conscious of the fact that it will not be only the materials that provide a solution but a combination of the software and whatever use the teachers make of it. It seems relatively unlikely that tablets, even those equipped with suitable programs and used appropriately by teachers, will be a miracle solution for learning difficulties. However, the introduction of new technology into classrooms has often improved teaching by complimenting existing tools. An example close to our subject is planar geometry. Dynamic geometry software has pre-existing drawing tools that allow the user to carry out a large number of drawings quickly. They also allow students to formulate conjectures. In the context of 3D geometry, we hypothesize that a tablet equipped with software based on appropriate interactions can advantageously complement existing tools by creating links between real objects from the tangible world, mental representations and their planar representations. We also believe that this link may be continuous thanks to intuitive interactions that allow the user to easily manipulate 3D objects and through this facilitate the creation of the object's mental representation. In the previous chapter, the acceptance of FINGERS was shown and it is now necessary to evaluate it in real teaching conditions in order to verify that it truly decreases students' cognitive load, thus allowing them to focus on learning 3D geometry.

In this chapter, we will discuss the partnerships that were developed in order to carry out these experiments, followed by the benefits of our approach in the case of problem solving as well as decreasing cognitive load during its use. Finally, we will present a longitudinal experiment that was carried out in two classrooms as well as the limits of this type of study.

## 4.1. Partnerships

In order to evaluate the educational benefits of our system in an ecological manner, it is important to initiate partnerships. It is also important to be able to exchange and prepare these experiments with teaching professionals, as their experienced feedback and relevant suggestions is a fundamental input and of precious help. Furthermore, during this evaluation period, we established privileged working relationships with two primary and two middle schools. Based on these exchanges, we took into account the recommendations and suggestions of the ESPÉ trainers (see section 4.1.2) as well as those from teachers who were particularly invested in both their job and the mathematics teachers' organizations.

### 4.1.1. *The schools in the field*

As our objective was to carry out evaluations on potential users of our software, that is students aged between 9 and 15 years, we judged it important to carry out ecological experiments. For this, we had to obtain authorization from the Rectory of the Nancy-Metz academy as well as from the Academy Inspections from the relevant department. We also had to find schools and teachers willing to accommodate us. We were able to establish partnerships with two primary and two secondary schools who both opened their doors to us and allowed us to carry out the experiments detailed in this chapter as well as some from the previous one. These four schools, in chronological order, are as follows:

– the "Les Gaudinettes" middle school in Marange-Silvange, that allowed us to carry out experiments with certain students from several of its classes;

– the primary and middle school "Notre Dame de Pont-à-Mousson" in Pont-à-Mousson, that allowed us to carry out experiments on students from both Years 5 and 7. This primary school is equipped with a mobile classroom with iPads which allowed us to use FINGERS and evaluate it under good experimental conditions with students;

– the applied school of "Sainte Thérèse" in Metz, which allowed us to carry out experiments on students from both Years 5 and 6.

We wish to thank these schools and their teachers who welcomed us, without whom these experiments could not have taken place.

## 4.1.2. The ESPÉ[1]

We also based our work on the many exchanges and suggestions given to us by trainers from the ESPÉ in Lorraine. The ESPÉ also allowed us, through its function as a trainer of future and current teachers, to carry out interviews on which we based our work and user-based approach.

### 4.1.3. Mathematics teachers' associations

Although our system was designed for students in a 3D geometry learning context, it would be of no use without taking into account the teaching professionals who are confronted on a daily basis with the realities of teaching and who are invested in continuously improving teaching in their classroom. Many of the professionals we consulted with belonged to two mathematics teachers' associations. The first, Sésamath, develops collaborative projects based on new technologies. Its members therefore have a high regard for the use of technology in the classroom and the exchanges that took place between us allowed us to better define the habits and needs of users. The second, the *Association des Professeurs de Mathématiques de l'Enseignement Public* (APMEP, or Association of Mathematics Teachers in Public Education) ensures that good practices are put in place, from kindergarten through to university.

We informally but actively collaborated with both of these structures and the many exchanges between us were profitable.

## 4.2. Limits

### 4.2.1. Ethical: the equality of chances for students

To evaluate and compare the impact of the use of FINGERS, teaching solids and the use of paper and pencils in learning 3D geometry, a comparison between groups using only one of these tools would have been the most appropriate methodology. We never, however, even considered this approach. Indeed, our sense of teaching ethics leads us to give each student the same learning opportunities. As such, we could not give one group less tools than the others during a three week long period, knowing experience that there was a strong possibility that this could lead to an unequal learning of the concept at play. Our results indeed show that if one group had access to only paper and pencils, they would have certainly been at a disadvantage.

---

1 Ecole Supérieure du Professorat et de l'Éducation or Graduate School for Teaching and Education

Furthermore, due to the decree of the 24th of August 2005 (France) relative to teaching aids in the success of primary and middle school students, teachers are obliged to do their best to ensure that everything is done to ensure that all students are able to meet their full potential:

> "Art. 4 – Educational dispositions put into place to ensure educational continuity, particularly throughout each cycle, take into account the needs of each student in order to allow the full development of their potential, as well as the objective of acquiring the elements of the common base of knowledge and fundamental competencies corresponding to their level of teaching" (from the decree of the 24th of August 2005, Article 4).

### 4.2.2. Practical: progression of the concepts throughout the year

To the ethical limits are added the practical ones. Indeed, a teacher cannot cover a program related to 3D geometry teaching twice throughout the school year. Therefore, a given class could only participate once in our evaluations and problems could easily lead to the whole experiment being delayed for a whole year. It is also essential to adapt to the teaching progression, as teachers gave a great deal of thought to the best point in the school year at which to teach a given concept. So, even if teachers have some degree of flexibility, the experimental opportunities were subject to time constraints. Furthermore, spiral progression through the curriculum, which allows students to return to concepts and which is more suitable to teaching, can complicate the set-up of these experiments. This type of progression makes the comparison of educational impact more difficult during the use of these tools. Between two teaching sessions of the same concept, students continue to think about it, seeing it in other areas and building their representation of what it can entail. Finally, it is also simpler to carry out these experiments in primary, rather than middle school, as in primary school the teacher manages their own classroom and in this way is more easily able to adapt to the experiments. Conversely, in middle school, a teacher is more constrained by their timetable and is unable to borrow hours from their colleagues.

### 4.3. Evaluation of problem-solving aids

Before carrying out in situ evaluations to measure the impact of our program on the learning of 3D geometry, we first wished to evaluate its use as a problem solving aid. Indeed, if it has no benefits when it comes to solving an exercise, but rather increases the complexity of the task for the students by increasing their cognitive load, it is unlikely it will benefit learning. To verify our hypotheses regarding the improvement of performance in problem solving, we carried out two experiments, one in the field and the other in the laboratory, which we shall now describe. Figure 4.1 summarizes the experimental plan for this chapter.

| Evaluation of problem solving aids (dec 2012) | Evaluation of the cognitive load (jan 2014) | Evaluation of teaching aids - Sainte Thérèse school (april-may 2014) |
|---|---|---|
| | Evaluation of teaching aids - Notre dame de Pont-à-Mousson school (dec 2013 - jan 2014) | |

**Figure 4.1.** *Educational teaching plan*

### 4.3.1. *In the field*

To evaluate the educational benefits of our group of interactions, we developed a "between groups" type of evaluation. This method consists of comparing the results obtained by several groups using a tool under the same conditions. The point here is not to determine whether the students have acquired competencies based on their use of the tablet or whether these were acquired in the long-term without the input of these technologies. The point was far more modest and was to see if our prototype is firstly an aide to problem solving exercises and secondly, if it at least allows students to rethink their initial representation when it is revealed to be false [BER 13b].

#### 4.3.1.1. *Participants*

We chose a group of 22 students (10 male and 12 female) aged between 10 and 15. These students were from the Sainte Thérèse Primary and Les Gaudinettes Middle schools. We chose this group with the help of teachers to ensure an accurate representation of different categories of students (those with difficulties, those with no particular difficulties and those more at ease). During the experiment, the initial group of students was divided into three sub-groups: a paper sub-group (GP, 8 students) using only paper and pencil; a tablet sub-group (GT, 7 students) using paper and tablets; a solids sub-group (GS, 7 students) using only paper and educational solids.

#### 4.3.1.2. *Task*

Each group of students solved two series of four mathematics exercises, both series being made up of similar exercises (Figure 4.2). The exercises were chosen because of the teaching benefits of giving students solid observational and manipulation skills as well as tasks from different point of view. Our choices were as follows:

– exercise 1: this exercise was modified and adapted from the 2011 Year 6 evaluations in which 40% of students were unable to correctly describe the cube and 50% of which could not describe the prism correctly;

– exercise 2: this exercise corresponds to Piaget's three mountain exercise that is described in Chapter 1;

– exercise 3: this exercise requires the manipulation of solids in order to count its painted faces one by one, a long and delicate process, or by developing a more rapid strategy. The suggested answers were followed by didactic analysis of the exercise and correspond to (as well as the correct answer) the more common errors that may be expected, for example counting the cubes and then multiplying the obtained number by 6 without taking into account the fact that the faces that were stuck together were not painted;

– exercise 4: this exercise requires finding the front, side and bottom views of a solid made up of nine cubes. Students could therefore not base their results on their previously obtained ones, as in exercise 1, and are forced to adapt their strategies depending on their position.

To summarize, exercises 1 and 3 require observational and manipulation skills from the students, whereas 2 and 4 are based on a decentralization.

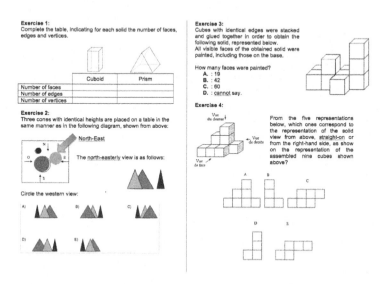

**Figure 4.2.** *Example of a series of four exercises given to students during their evaluation*

### 4.3.1.3. *Material*

For the group equipped with a tablet, experiments were carried out using iPads 2, on which four test programs were installed based on FINGERS and corresponding to each exercise of the chosen series (Figure 4.3). The group using solids had access to educational solids provided by ESPÉ (Figure 4.3) and corresponding to each exercise.

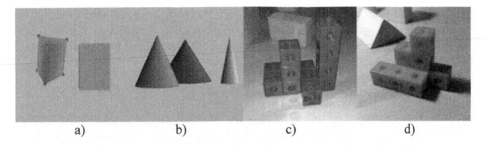

a)             b)                c)                d)

**Figure 4.3.** *Material used in the experiments: a) exercise 1;*
*b) exercise 2; c) exercise 3; d) exercise 4*

### 4.3.1.4. *Experimental plan*

The experiments were carried out over three separate days over the course of a week. The first two days were successive and the third was exactly a week after the first. The experiments were split into three sessions, the first taking place on the first day and the other two on the third day:

– pre-test (session 1): all the students carried out a test made up of four exercises, using only a sheet of paper and a pen. This session was used as a diagnostic in group construction. The exercises were corrected without the students and their results were not communicated to them in order to limit their bias. The test was followed by a questionnaire which gathered students' opinions regarding the ease, use and fun of each exercise as well as the ease of interpretation of the representations in perspective of the solids;

– test (session 2): the students were separated into three groups: one using only pen and paper (GP , 8 students), one using tablets equipped with our prototype (GT, 7 students) and one using the educational solids corresponding to the different exercises (GS, 7 students). The three groups then carried out a second similar test (with 4 exercises) that was the same for all three groups. In order to create the groups, we took two factors into account: the typology of the errors during the first test and the age of the student. Statistical analysis showed an absence of any significant differences between the three groups. Once again, these exercises were corrected without the presence of the students and their results were not communicated to them;

– post-test (session 3): we asked the students to correct, if needed, the exercises they had just carried out during the test. The conditions were the same as during the test. A questionnaire, identical to the initial one, was then distributed and completed by the students. Finally, we carried out post-experimental interviews.

The second day of the experiment was only for the group using the tablets. After a three-minute presentation regarding the program, they participated in two ten-minute-long training sessions with the prototype using unrelated tasks to the pre-test, test or post-test.

Table 4.1 summarizes our experimental protocol.

| Group | Pre-test | | Test | Post-test |
|---|---|---|---|---|
| | Monday | Tuesday | Monday (one week later) | |
| Paper group | 4 exercises, un-corrected (no groups formed) – Sheet of paper – Questionnaire | | 4 paper exercises | Correction and questionnaire |
| Tablet group | | 2 training sessions with FINGERS | 4 tablet exercises | |
| Solid group | | | 4 solid exercises | |

**Table 4.1.** *Summary of the experimental protocol*

## 4.3.1.5. *Results and discussion*

Figure 4.4 shows the success rate of the pre-test, test and post-test. The three initial groups do not present any significant differences during the pre-test (X-squared = 2.4107, df = 2, p-value = 0.2996). We may note that the only group with any significant difference between the pre-test and post-test is the group that used the tablets. The paper group is nearly constant (X-squared = 0, df = 1, p-value = 1), the tablet group significantly increases its success rate (X-squared = 4.6667, df = 1, p-value = 0.03075) and the solids group decreases it slightly (X-squared = 0.6562, df = 1, p-value = 0.4179). The latter two of these results surprised us a lot, particularly in the case of the solids. Interviews with students highlighted three main reasons as follows:

– students experienced difficulties linking solids or real scenes with their paper representations. This posed a problem for four students;

– certain students were not used to using solids in order to solve exercises. For example, during exercise 2, two students rotated the base on which the three mountains were set rather than moving themselves around it. After a short time, they were unable to orient themselves. This confirms that these two actions are truly two separate tasks for the student from a learning point of view;

– students from the solids group were the most confident in their answers and 6 of them did not attempt to correct their work during the post-test.

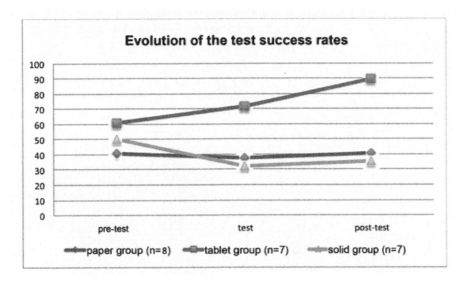

**Figure 4.4.** *Success rate in percentages for each group and session*

We were able to observe that during the test, the solid and tablet groups most often used the tools that were available to them in order to look for answers to the exercises rather than to check them (GS: 57%; GT: 75%). Furthermore, the tablet group more often carried out manipulation via the prototype than the solid group. During the interviews, the tablet group students explained that they were not confident enough and that they were concentrating hard due to the fact that this was their first use of the prototype to solve problems. They also underlined the fact that they were able to rotate around solids in a realistic manner and that when they stopped they had a good representation of the plane, simplifying their identification of the correct answer, particularly for exercises 2 and 4. We also noted a significant evolution in the typology of errors for the tablet group, since 91% of them were due to pre-test visualization and only 50% for the post-test. A direct comparison of the representations of solids on tablets and on paper explains this difference.

It seems therefore that the use of the tablet equipped with our prototype is an aide to solving exercises for our sample test. It is important, however, to note that there are limits to this. Indeed, the benefits of the tablet and prototype are not the same for all exercises. Using, for example, the results of exercise 1, based on national testing of Year 6s, it was of nearly no help. In a very classical type of exercise, the students tended to use their pre-existing knowledge of manipulation and visualization tools. This observation leads us to think that the use of FINGERS would be of more use for investigative-type exercises rather than for direct applications of knowledge. Even if the group of students who used the tablets found them more useful for solving exercises, there was not any significant difference between the other two groups (including the paper group) (Figure 4.5).

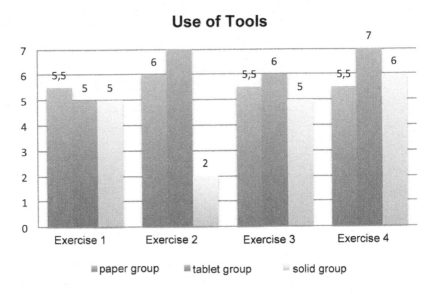

**Figure 4.5.** *Evaluation by the students of the use of their tools on a scale of 0 to 7 (median)*

Feedback from students regarding our group of interactions was positive. They found the implemented movements to be adapted to solving exercises and the suggested situations, as shown by Table 4.2. ANOVA-type analyses showed a significant increase in participants' opinions between the pre-test and the post-test on four points of the questionnaire: ease ($F_{2,19} = 8.511$, $p = 0.008$), use ($F_{2,19} = 5.090$, $p = 0.036$), fun ($F_{2,19} = 8.312$, $p = 0.010$) of each exercise and the ease of interpretation of the solids' representations in perspective ($F_{2,19} = 31.94$, $p < 0.0001$). However, it is interesting to note that students from the tablet group did not find the exercises to be more easy, interesting or fun than the other groups by using the tablet. Indeed, our analysis shows no significant differences between the groups. This last point, added to the helpful impression the tools made, shows that it is not the material that creates the impression of ease, use or fun of the exercises, but the fact that the second series of exercises was similar to the first. This is confirmed by the ANOVA analysis, which showed no significant difference in opinions between the different exercises ($F_{6,57} = 1.83$, $p = 0.108$). We were surprised that students did not find it at least more fun to be using iPads for solving mathematical problems. During the interviews they explained that a mathematics exercise will always be the same, with or without the use of a tablet (or solids). This remark leads us to think that any attraction linked to the use of technology is fairly weak and may be explained by the fact that this type of technology is now quite common.

|  | Exercise 1 | Exercise 2 | Exercise 3 | Exercise 4 |
|---|---|---|---|---|
| Adapted interactions | 6 (2.5) | 7 (1.5) | 7 (1) | 7 (1) |

**Table 4.2.** *User feedback on the adaptation of interactions to the exercises and situations suggested on the Likert eight-point scale (median and interquartile)*

To conclude, our group of interactions obtained a significant increase in results when compared with the two other types of tools used, that is educational solids and the traditional pen and paper. Added to the evolution of the typology of errors, we noted that the interactions are an aid to problem solving. However, we did note that these benefits are not the same for all exercises and that new experiments should be carried out in order to determine exactly which problem typologies would be most relevant to the use of a tool such as FINGERS.

### 4.3.1.6. *Limits*

Other than the limit we have just described in our conclusion to problem typology, we encountered another important limit at an organizational and logistical level. By making the choice of carrying out between group experimentation, we restricted the number of users in each group. Indeed, the number of participants for each group was below ten. These low numbers are explained by the difficulty associated with bringing together both primary and middle school students between the ages of 10 and 15 years from different schools.

### 4.3.2. Laboratory (EEG)

After having shown that our group of interactions facilitates problem solving in 3D geometry for students, we shall now study its impact on the cognitive charge during problem solving [BER 14]. Unlike all the other experiments described in this book, this is the only one to be carried out with adults, for a simple reason: we did not have the materials necessary to carry it out with children as described in the "materials" section.

Consequently, we were not able to conclude from it any directly transferable statements to our targeted audience. However, it is important to us to present these results as they make up a significant research pathway and allow us to formulate interesting hypotheses for further research. Before describing and detailing the results, we shall begin with a brief state-of-the-art.

#### 4.3.2.1. A brief state-of-the-art

In this section, we shall begin with [CHA 07]'s definition of the cognitive load, which is as follows:

"Corresponding to a quantity, a measure of the intensity of the cognitive process engaged in by a particular individual, possessing certain knowledge and resources, to carry out a certain task, in a certain way, in a certain environment".

The cognitive load theory is based on the fact that working memory is limited and can only take a restricted amount of information, unlike our long-term memory [BAD 86, SWE 88]. So, if it is too highly in demand, the cognitive load becomes too increased, which consequently leads to failure of the task or erroneous memorization in long-term memory.

According to Sweller, there are three main types of cognitive load (Figure 4.6):

– *intrinsic cognitive load:* the inherent cognitive load of an activity linked to the complexity of its content and interactive elements;

– *extrinsic cognitive load*: the cognitive load linked to the manner in which information is presented. It is dependent on the choices made by the presenter and can be minimized by eliminating redundant or attention dispersing elements;

– *germane cognitive load*: the cognitive load that favors the transfer of knowledge into long-term memory. During repeated encounters with the same educational material, it allows for the creation of mental representations that favor learning.

To conclude, the intrinsic cognitive load cannot be modified, the extrinsic cognitive load must be minimized and the germane cognitive load must be favored.

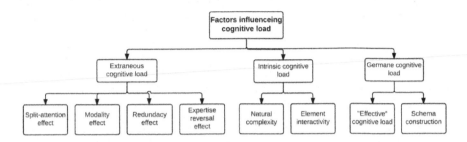

**Figure 4.6.** *Different types of cognitive load according to [SWE 05] and the factors linked to them*

Measuring the cognitive load during a task is a difficult procedure. According to [CAO 09], measurement techniques of the cognitive load must have the following characteristics: sensible, with diagnostic capacity, selective, un-intrusive and easily implementable. There are three main approaches to measuring the cognitive load [JON 10]:

– *subjective methods*: based on subjective evaluations of tasks after which the participant estimates the mental effort through a questionnaire on a nine-point scale [PAA 92] ;

– *dual task realization methods*: based on cognitive resources available for carrying out secondary tasks. The principle is to introduce a secondary and less costly task in parallel to the main one. In this methodology, poor performance in the secondary task is considered to be due to a cognitive surcharge in carrying out the main task;

– *physiological methods*: based on the recording of physiological parameters such as cardiac rhythm, blood pressure [FRE 05], pupil dilatation [PAA 03] or even electro-encephalogram (EEG).

Subjective methods and carrying out dual tasks are both interesting in measuring cognitive load but the methods of this physiological measurement are more relevant to objective measurements of this charge [HAN 88]. Nowadays, easy-to-use EEG systems exist, both light and cordless [JOH 11].

4.3.2.2. *Measure of visuospatial capacity, attention and working memory*

The complex figure test by Rey-Osterrieth (ROCF) is a neuropsychological evaluation in which participants are asked to reproduce a complex drawing (Figure 4.7), first by copying it, then from memory. Many different cognitive abilities are required in order to successfully carry out the task and the test thereby evaluates different functions such as visuospatial capacity, memorization, attention, anticipation and working memory. The two conditions used in the ROCF are as follows:

– *copying*: the participant receives a white sheet of paper, a pencil and the figure that is to be copied, placed in front of them (Figure 4.7), with the task of reproducing it to their best ability. The test is not time-limited but is timed and taken into account;

– *immediate reproduction*: after a short break of three minutes, the participant is asked to reproduce the figure from memory.

The notation of the drawings carried out by the participants is based on a 36-point system. The same notation criteria is applied to both drawings. Each notation point is based on precision and placement criteria.

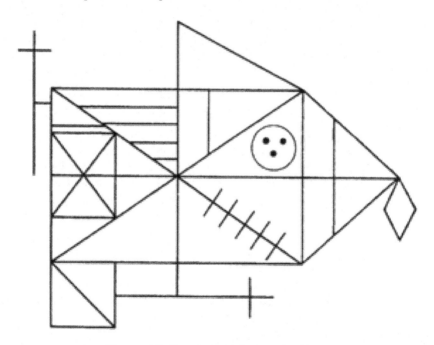

**Figure 4.7.** *Rey-Osterrieth complex figure*

### 4.3.2.3. *Participants*

In order to carry out this experiment, we recruited 17 participants. All of them were female and Human and Social Studies students at the University of Lorraine. They had all previously used a touchscreen tablet and were regular users of multi-touch devices (smartphone or other). Following the Rey-Osterrieth figure test, we verified that there were no significant differences in visuospatial capacity, memorization or attention between the participants.

### 4.3.2.4. *Material*

In the handover, the participants were equipped with the following:

– a sheet of paper and a pencil;

– a Polydrons kit, a teaching material for working on solids and the concept of nets (Figure 4.8);

– an iPad equipped with FINGERS.

**Figure 4.8.** *Teaching materials used: polydrons.*
*(Photograph by Nevit Dilmen, CC BY SA 3.0)*

In order to carry out measurements of the cognitive load, the participants were equipped with an EEG system of the Advanced Brain Monitoring type (Figure 4.9(a)). Advanced Brain Monitoring (ABM) is an implemented and integrated material and software solution for the real time acquisition and analysis of EEGs (Figures 4.9(b) and 4.9(c)). The system includes a wireless EEG helmet that is easily installed. ABM has developed an analytical approach in order to identify and quantify cognitive state changes. This technique allows the simultaneous selection of several EEG characteristics in different regions of the brain, leading to a high sensitivity and a specific method for monitoring neural cognitive signals, whether as real time or later data analyses.

This system has been used in several studies in order to identify somnolence-vigilance states as well as cognitive load during both simple and complex tasks [BER 04, BER 07].

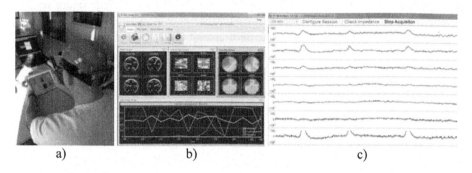

a)                      b)                                      c)

**Figure 4.9.** *Example of the obtained data using the ABM system:*
*a) the test system as installed; b) monitoring screen; c) EEG recordings.*
*For a color version of this figure, see www.iste.co.uk/bertolo/geometry.zip*

### 4.3.2.5. Task

Each participant needed to solve three 3D geometry problems, with each problem being solved three times, using a different tool each time (paper-pencil, polydrons, FINGERS). The three problems were as follows:

– draw a cube in perspective;

– draw another perspective of the cube after rotation;

– draw a net of the cube, different to the classical cross-shaped one.

### 4.3.2.6. Experimental plan

The experimental plan was separated into five phases:

– *Phase 1*: Each participant was invited to sit in a quiet room and the experiment was explained to them along with its aim, that is the study of the strategies used by adults in order to solve 3D geometry problems.

– *Phase 2*: Each participant was equipped with the wireless helmet and the sensors were positioned on the following zones: F3-F4, C3-C4, Cz-PO, F3-Cz, Fz-C3, Fz-PO.

– *Phase 3*: Each participant carried out the Rey-Osterrieth complex figure test.

– *Phase 4*: After verification of the impedance tests from each of the 10 sensors, each participant completed three system calibration tasks:

- the vigilance test vigilance of the three choices (3C-VT) consists in distinguishing between three shapes 20 minutes after the shapes were shown;

- detection of a visual target on a computer screen with open eyes;

- detection of a sound (left/right) with closed eyes.

These three tasks are commonly used during neurocognitive tests.

– *Phase 5*: Each participant solved three 3D geometry problems under three conditions that corresponded to the three available tools (pencil-paper, polydrons and FINGERS). Figure 4.10 shows the three handover conditions. The testing order for each condition was counterbalanced in order to avoid any ordering effect and any potential decrease in vigilance and attention.

In our analysis, we took into account the following three factors:

– the participant's success in the task for each of the three exercises;

– the time required (in seconds) to solve each problem;

– the cognitive load when solving each of the three exercises.

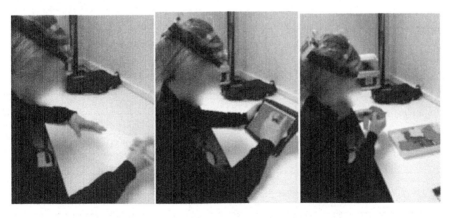

**Figure 4.10.** *Problem solving under three different conditions*

### 4.3.2.7. *Results and discussion*

This experiment, carried out with the previously described 17 participants, allowed us to conclude the following interesting points:

– Table 4.3 shows that there is no significant difference in success rates for the three conditions. The majority of participants (between 82.5% and 100%) were able to solve the three 3D geometry problems regardless of the tool (paper-pencil, polydrons, FINGERS). These results are not surprising when one considers the simplicity of these tasks for adults;

– however, the tool in question had a significant impact on the time required in order to carry out the task and solve the problem (Table 4.3). ANOVA analysis shows that the time required increases significantly during the use of paper and pencils ($F_{2,14} = 8.12$, $p < 0.005$). There were no other significant results;

– Table 4.4 shows that depending on the problem, the cognitive state changes. For the two simpler exercises (drawing a cube in perspective and drawing another perspective of this cube after rotation), no matter what tool is used, the most common cognitive state is low engagement, corresponding to a low cognitive load. For the more complicated exercise (construction of a different cube net to the classical cross shape), no matter which tool was used, the most common cognitive state was high engagement, corresponding to a high cognitive load;

– finally, ANOVA analysis reveals that the cognitive load decreases significantly for the more complicated exercise when FINGERS is used ($F_{2,14} = 10.25$, $p < 0.001$).

| | | 3D geometry exercises | | |
|---|---|---|---|---|
| *Condition* | *Criteria* | *Cube representation* | *Cube representation after rotation* | *Cube net* |
| *Paper-pencil* | Score (%) | 17 (100%) | 17 (100%) | 14 (82,5%) |
| | Time | 49 | 133 | 174 |
| *Polydrons* | Score (%) | 17 (100%) | 17 (100%) | 15 (88,2%) |
| | Time | 82 | 22 | 55 |
| *FINGERS* | Score (%) | 17 (100%) | 17 (100%) | 15 (88,2%) |
| | Time | 11 | 4 | 13 |

**Table 4.3.** *Test results: success rate and duration (in seconds) for each condition*

| Condition | Criteria | 3D geometry exercises | | |
|---|---|---|---|---|
| | | Cube representation | Cube representation after rotation | Cube net |
| Paper-pencil | Somnolence | 0 | 0 | 0 |
| | Distraction | 0.079 | 0.014 | 0.023 |
| | Low eng. | 0.498 | 0.386 | 0.353 |
| | High eng. | 0.365 | 0.288 | 0.812 |
| Polydrons | Somnolence | 0 | 0 | 0 |
| | Distraction | 0.011 | 0.005 | 0.016 |
| | Low eng. | 0.658 | 0.751 | 0.457 |
| | High eng. | 0.346 | 0.254 | 0.624 |
| FINGERS | Somnolence | 0 | 0 | 0 |
| | Distraction | 0.012 | 0.002 | 0.009 |
| | Low eng. | 0.521 | 0.569 | 0.341 |
| | High eng. | 0.401 | 0.274 | 0.401 |

**Table 4.4.** *Measurement of the probability of work charge where the highest probability shows a high cognitive load. For a color version of this table, see www.iste.co.uk/bertolo/geometry.zip*

The results obtained during this experiment showed that the cognitive load decreased significantly when FINGERS was used but only in the case of complex 3D geometry problems. This also implies that our program has no impact on cognitive load when a problem only requires low cognitive engagement. Furthermore, our previous experiment shows a significant increase in results when our group of interactions is used for solving 3D geometry problems. In accordance with Chanquoy's definition of cognitive load, it would seem that 3D geometry problems that adults find simple are only partially or not at all so for students who are in the midst of forming their spatial representations and structuring of space. Therefore, these latter results explain this significant increase in problem-solving results which is that the group of interactions used in FINGERS minimizes the cognitive load when solving these problems. It will be important and interesting to carry out this experiment again, using children aged between 9 and 15 years.

In accordance with the principles set out by Oviatt [OVI 06] to minimize the cognitive load in a human-centered design, we have suggested the following three hypotheses formulating how FINGERS is beneficial:

1) it takes into account the "natural" and intuitive interaction modes of users;

2) it minimizes any potential sources of difficulty on a linguistic and behavioral level;

3) it takes into account working habits in a familiar environment.

## 4.4. Evaluation of the benefits in learning 3D geometry

The previous experiments all brought together the required elements for an evaluation of the benefits of our gestural grammar. Indeed, we know that the interactions were well accepted by students, that they significantly increased success rates during problem solving, and that the use of FINGERS, in complex problems, minimized the cognitive load (in adults). We shall now present the experiments developed in order to evaluate any potential benefits to learning, implying a longer term and more ecological study, through immersion into one or several classrooms.

### 4.4.1. *Participants*

To carry out this experiment, we went into the Year 5 classrooms of two different schools with which we were partnered. In total, the experiment was carried out on 48 students. None of the participants were colorblind. In both schools, the students were already using tablets. During the experiment, the classes were divided into three groups.

#### 4.4.1.1. *École Notre Dame in Pont-à-Mousson (school A)*

The class from school A was made up of 25 students, 15 male and 10 female, all between the ages of 9 and 10. The school was equipped with a mobile classroom containing 30 iPad 2s. Furthermore, all students had already used a tablet, but only in the context of internet research for school.

#### 4.4.1.2. *École Sainte Thérèse (school B)*

The class from school B was made up of 23 students, of which 11 were male and 12 were female, all aged between 9 and 11 years. The school was not equipped with either a mobile classroom or tablets for students, but the teachers were equipped with Microsoft Surfaces that the students were encouraged to use during presentations.

### 4.4.2. *Material and experimental conditions*

During this study, FINGERS was set up on the iPad 2s of the mobile classroom of school A and our laboratory's iPad Airs for school B (Figure 4.11(a) and (c)). Depending on the week and the groups, students were given access to lettered wooden solids (Figure 4.1(b)) in order to be able to identify them without needing to know the shape's mathematical name, as well as to be able to carry out some of the exercises. They were also given access to boxes of polydrons (Figure 4.11(d)) during their work on nets.

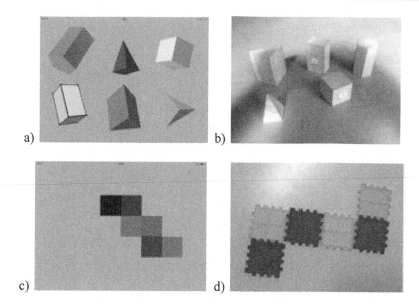

**Figure 4.11.** *Materials used during the experiments with both classes: a) and c) are screenshots from FINGERS; b) wooden blocks; d) polydrons. For a color version of this table, see www.iste.co.uk/bertolo/geometry.zip*

Throughout the experiments, all the sessions were designed in collaboration with the teacher from school A, always with regard given to the educational outlook and the Year 5 curriculum, which set the two following objectives:

– recognizing, describing and naming regular solids: cubes, cuboids, prisms;

– recognizing or completing a net of a cube or cuboid.

During the duplication of this experiment with school B, the sessions from school A were carried out without any modifications and in the same material organization conditions as well as with the same instructions.

During each of the sessions where the students used different tools (paper-pencil, solids, FINGERS), we timed each student over each exercise. We also took detailed notes, particularly in regard to any didactic problems that were encountered as well as any strategies that the students developed in order to solve the problems, with or without the use of a tool. During the sessions using different tools, as the students were separated into three groups, we set up three separate classrooms in both schools in order to not distract the students from other groups with different tools. The students were all together during the presentation and institutionalization of the lesson.

### 4.4.3. *Experimental plan*

This study was carried out over two eight-week-long periods:

1) December 2013–January 2014;

2) April 2014–May 2014.

During these two periods, each experiment with the students lasted four weeks.

The second period was an exact duplication of the experimental plan of the first, therefore we shall not describe it again.

Each period was divided into two sections:

1) Sessions with the students and weekly evaluations over three weeks;

2) Final evaluation in order to monitor learning five weeks after the first section.

#### 4.4.3.1. *Description of the first section:*

On the first day, we carried out a diagnostic test. Based on this and using the help of the classroom teacher, we split the class into three equivalent groups in terms of knowledge and competency in 3D geometry. We took into account the results and error typology of the pre-test as well as the teacher's point of view, as someone who knows the students and knows which groups to avoid forming.

Each week, every group used a single tool (pencil-paper, solids and polydrons, FINGERS) in order to help them with the 3D geometry sessions, such that, at the end of this first section, each group would have used all the tools.

At the beginning of each week, we evaluated the students with paper and pencil tests in the same way. We shall call these the pre-tests and those at the end of the week the post-tests. In a given week, each group had three exercise sessions with a tool. At the start of each week, before any of the exercises sessions took place, the group that was to use FINGERS had one 15-minute training session in which to learn how to use the software. This training session was unrelated to the exercises and concepts to be covered that week.

At the end of each week, the students who used FINGERS completed a questionnaire in order to gather their opinions of the software, the ease of use as well as the relevance of permanently having access to it. We also carried out weekly interviews with the students in order to gather their impressions.

During the three weeks of lessons, the following concepts were tackled:

– *week 1*: visualization of solids. Students were asked to count the number of faces, edges and vertices of various solids. They also had to determine the shapes of different faces of the solid in order to be able to distinguish them and then class them based on their characteristics;

– *week 2*: discovery of the concept of a net. Students implicitly discovered what a cube's net is as no definition of one was given. They were required to find all the nets of a cube as well as recognizing its simpler ones;

– *week 3*: work on nets, being able to identify and complete cube nets. Students were asked to recognize more complex cube nets or simple ones of other polyhedrons. They also had to complete cube nets.

Between the first and second sections of the experiment, the students had a four week period (of which two weeks were vacation) during which they did not carry out any work linked to what they achieved during these three weeks of work on 3D geometry.

The second section therefore took place five weeks after the first. All the students took the same final evaluation, carried out with only paper and pencil. After this, the whole class took part in a debriefing and we also asked each participant which tool they preferred to use during the course of the experiment.

Table 4.5 summarizes the experimental protocol used.

| Week | Group 1 | Group 2 | Group 3 |
|---|---|---|---|
| 1 | Diagnostic tests and group formation | | |
| | iPad | Solids / Polydrons | Paper |
| 2 | Evaluation of learning / Diagnostic tests | | |
| | Solids / Polydrons | Paper | iPad |
| 3 | Evaluation of learning / Diagnostic tests | | |
| | Paper | iPad | Solids / Polydrons |
| | Evaluation of learning | | |
| 5 weeks later | Final evaluation | | |
| | Debriefing with students | | |

**Table 4.5.** *Summary of the experimental protocol put into place with the two classes*

## 4.4.4. *Results and discussion*

### 4.4.4.1. *Educational results*

Figures 4.12, 4.13 and 4.14 show the success rates of the pre- and post-tests as well as the difference in rates between the two depending on the tools and weeks of the two schools. We note that all the groups obtained better results in the post-test than in the pre-test, regardless of the school, which is not always the case as their teachers confirmed. Table 4.6 shows that FINGERS lead to significant improvement in results between the pre- and post-test four times out of six, whereas for the other tools, this was only the case two times out of six (paper–pencil and solids/polydrons).

| Week | School | FINGERS | Solids | Paper–pencil |
|---|---|---|---|---|
| 1 | A | $X^2 = 4.2784$<br>df = 1<br>p-val. = **0.0386** | $X^2 = 0.2876$<br>df = 1<br>p-val. = 0.5917 | $X^2 = 0.1036$<br>df = 1<br>p-val. = 0.7476 |
| | B | $X^2 = 0.0154$<br>df = 1<br>p-val. = 0.9012 | $X^2 = 0.4822$<br>df = 1<br>p-val. = 0.4874 | $X^2 = 2.2073$<br>df = 1<br>p-val. = 0.1374 |
| 2 | A | $X^2 = 20.1446$<br>df = 1<br>p-val. = **7.18e-06** | $X^2 = 7.5142$<br>df = 1<br>p-val. = **0.006121** | $X^2 = 26.4281$<br>df = 1<br>p-val. = **2.735e-07** |
| | B | $X^2 = 5.0258$<br>df = 1<br>p-val. = **0.02497** | $X^2 = 0.9978$<br>df = 1<br>p-val. = 0.3178 | $X^2 = 27.9565$<br>df = 1<br>p-val. = **1.241e-07** |
| 3 | A | $X^2 = 4.816$<br>df = 1<br>p-val. = **0.0282** | $X^2 = 5.9196$<br>df = 1<br>p-val. = **0.01497** | $X^2 = 1.9573$<br>df = 1<br>p-val. = 0.1618 |
| | B | $X^2 = 2.2578$<br>df = 1<br>p-val. = 0.1329 | $X^2 = 2.8885$<br>df = 1<br>p-val. = 0.08922 | $X^2 = 1.9056$<br>df = 1<br>p-val. = 0.1675 |

**Table 4.6.** *Comparison of the success rates at the pre-test and post-test for each week (Khi$^2$, significant values in bold)*

### 4.4.4.1.1. Week 1

At the end of the first week, the students from school A explained to us that it was easier to count the edges and vertices as they appear when the solid is selected. Furthermore, they enjoyed having the possibility to be able to select the solid as a "metal wire" representation, leaving only the edges showing. This technique was also adopted by students from school B. They also enjoyed using FINGERS and found it useful for counting the characteristic elements of solids. In the questionnaires there were many remarks of the following type (mistakes have been deliberately left):

"It helped me because it highlights the edges and the vertices and the face".

"A bit, what helped me the most is when the solid was invisible as I was able to count the edges and vertices".

"Yes, a lot because we can more easily see the solids and for the edges, faces... it's very useful".

"Yes it helped me. Because there are effects we can't see in reality".

During the first week in school B, the absence of any significant progression with FINGERS and the other tools can be explained by the already good results at the pre-test. Figure 4.12 shows that the pre-test results of school B are nearly as high as school A's post-test results. This difference shows that generally, school B's students already had knowledge relating to solids. Their progression margin was thus reduced and did not lead to any significant increases.

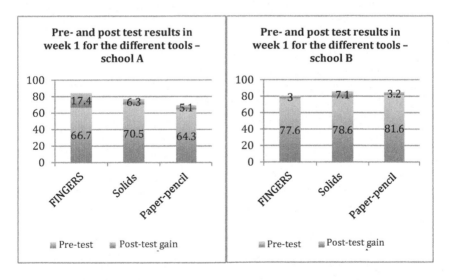

**Figure 4.12.** *Results of both pre and post-tests based on the tool used as well as the percentage between the two during week 1*

### 4.4.4.1.2. Week 2

The second week corresponded to the discovery of polyhedron nets. The ones the students were required to identify were simple and some were able to identify them without the use of the tools to which they had access. These two elements are explained by the fact that the results of the pre- and post-tests were very close for all three tools in school A. In school B, the group using paper and pencil obtained particularly low results at the pre-test, explaining their strong increase in results over the week. This was also the case in school A. We also noted that the only group that did not exhibit any significant increase in results was the group using solids from school B. One of the possible explanations for this is linked to the lack of familiarity with solid manipulation, particularly for polyhedrons. Indeed, whereas school A had access to a lot of educational materials, we had to provide a box of polydrons for weeks 2 and 3's sessions in school B. Consequently, students discovered polydrons and their manipulation at this time. This last point may have influenced the students' concentration levels and the strategies they chose to use. Based on this hypothesis and knowing that students from both schools did not know FINGERS, they still significantly improved their results, which lead us to think that learning to use FINGERS is more efficient than polydrons. Finally, we note that with the exception of this group, all of them managed over a 75% success rate at the post-test (Figure 4.13).

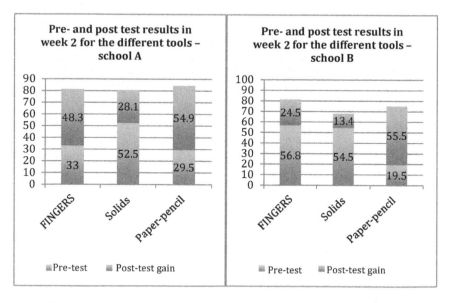

**Figure 4.13.** *Results of both pre- and post-tests based on the tool used as well as the percentage between the two during week 2*

## 4.4.4.1.3. Week 3

During the third week, the nets the students were required to use and identify were more complex and less classical. Students were thereby required to use the tools they had access to in order to solve the problems. We noted that from this point, the use of polydrons and solids as well as FINGERS all allowed the students to obtain better results than paper and pencil for school A. For school B, the results were the other way around, where the group using paper and pencils obtained the best results. We may however note that only the groups using FINGERS and solids obtained any significant increase in results during the post-test. Interviews with the participants suggest that FINGERS enabled them to easily manipulate the nets and faces of the solids. They underlined that "unfolding" a cube and seeing an initial net was a good starting point for researching and finding other nets. In the questionnaire, the following remarks are once again common:

"Yes, because it helped us construct our cube pattern".

"Yes, it helped me because the iPad can open and close the cubes".

"Yes, because we could fold the patterns, turn them in all directions".

"Yes, because we don't need tape and don't need scissors it's faster".

"Yes, because for the nets we could fold them and see if it was a cube pattern…"

At the end of these three weeks, we note that over the six sessions carried out with each tool, the use of FINGERS leads to significant results twice as often as solids or paper and pencil. Furthermore, we timed the exercises carried out by each participant. As such, we noted that at the start of the week, the group using FINGERS required nearly twice as much time than the group using solids in order to carry out the exercises. However, by the end of the week, the gap between the group using FINGERS and the one using the solids was less than a minute, showing a rapid assimilation of the use of this software.

Five weeks later, during the second section, we carried out a final test. We saw no significant differences in terms of the acquisition of the competencies. Except for two students from school A and one from school B, all others acquired the competencies during the first section of the experiment. Figure 4.15 shows the results of the final test from the students from both schools.

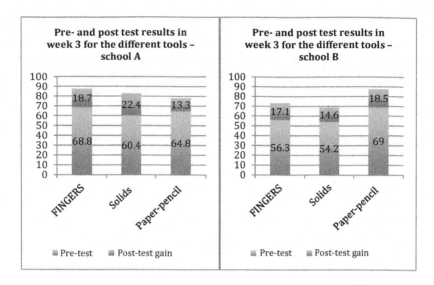

Figure 4.14. *Results of both pre- and post-tests based on the tool used as well as the percentage between the two during week 3*

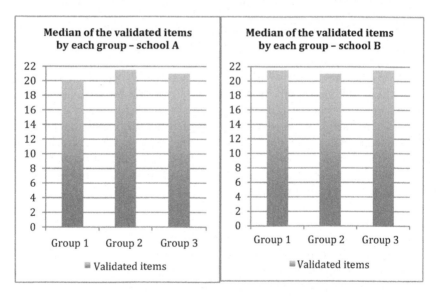

Figure 4.15. *Median of the validated items (out of 22) of the final test for each group*

During the discussions with students, they remarked that they found all the tools to be complimentary to each other. Indeed, five students thought that the use of the educational solids following the use of FINGERS helped them develop a better understanding of what they were doing by solving the exercises. Conversely, seven students considered that the use of FINGERS after the use of solids enabled them to answer more easily during the paper post-test. They explained that with FINGERS they could anticipate their actions more, helping them in their work on planar representations on paper. Six students also remarked that they particularly appreciated being able to independently verify the validity of their answers when working on nets. Amongst others, this last point motivated them to search for other cube nets.

The significant increase in the success rate of exercise solving during the post-test, after the use of FINGERS, combined with the high success rates at the final test, five weeks later, shows an educational benefit to the learning of 3D geometry. During our experiment, FINGERS was more useful than solids or polydrons, and seems to have been complimentary to the other tools used.

### 4.4.4.2. User feedback

The answers to the weekly questionnaires, interviews and debriefings in both schools suggested to us that the participants see FINGERS and the interactions it used positively. Figure 4.16 summarizes the answers given by the students in the questionnaire. They generally found that the software was helpful in solving the problems and that it was simple to use. Indeed, they would like to use it on a permanent basis in the classroom.

Furthermore, out of the 48 students from both schools:

– 31 preferred the use of FINGERS. The main reason for this was the ability to use it easily with their fingers. They found its use to be fun and enjoyable. For them, it was easier to see the solids in "metal wire" representation and to create patterns using it;

– 11 preferred the use of solids and polydrons. The main reason for this was the ability to actually, rather than virtually, move them;

– 6 preferred the use of paper and pencil. The main reason for this was there preference for writing and drawing. They also indicated that they were able to count the edges by marking them off progressively on the paper planar representation of the object.

Finally, it is interesting to note that one student from school B managed to use FINGERS and enjoyed doing so while having both arms in slings. Even if the manipulation of the software was not obvious to her, it was easier than that of polydrons which required slotting together, or for the paper and pencil, scissors and glue. This observation opens up possibilities for the use of such software, in the inclusion of special needs children.

During the final interview with each of the two classroom teachers who participated in our experiments, we received positive feedback. Indeed, the two teachers found that students had more easily and better acquired the knowledge and competencies linked to the concepts at play compared with their experience with previous classes. They suggested carrying out a more in-depth investigation by focusing on the benefits of our software on struggling students. Again, according to them, it seemed that these students experiences fewer problems during the learning of these concepts. Finally, they asked if it would be possible to continue using this software as they found it very useful. They indicated that FINGERS enabled a complimentary approach through an alternative method of visualization and manipulation of solids.

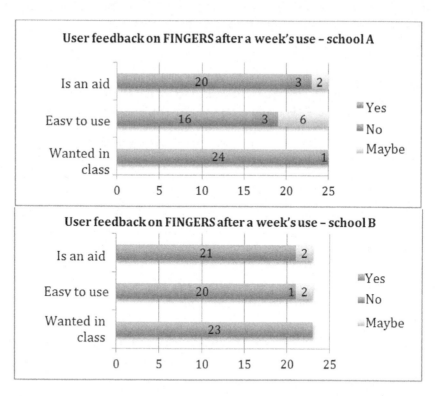

**Figure 4.16.** *User feedback on FINGERS after a week's use for each group*

## 4.5. Partial conclusions

In this chapter, we showed that FINGERS and the group of interactions it uses significantly increase problem-solving results. We noted that this increase is even greater when the problems relate to student-lead investigation. It would be interesting to define the most relevant use cases. In parallel to our first experiments evaluating the impact of FINGERS on learning 3D geometry, we measured the influence of our software on cognitive load, compared with the use of traditional solids and of paper and pen. In an adult sample, it appeared that FINGERS decreased the cognitive load in cases where it is used to solve complex problems. It would be interesting to carry this experiment out again with our target audience. Finally, we were able to see that during two identical experiments carried out with two Year 5 classes, the groups that used FINGERS significantly increased their results twice as often than those using solids or paper and pen. During these evaluations, the students found that a tablet was complimentary to the other tools available. The final test results, five weeks after the start of this experiment, testify to the acquisition of knowledge and competencies that the students worked on during this time. At this stage we can therefore conclude that FINGERS facilitates the learning of 3D geometry through the lowering of the cognitive load and a manipulatory and visual approach which is different as well as complimentary to those already in use: "Yes, with this program, it's a lot easier because we don't really have to physically manipulate anything and it's more visual".

# Conclusion and Perspectives

Mobile devices, in particular smartphones and digital tablets, have become widely used and popular over recent years. These new popular devices are integrated with many electrical components, such as sensors (gyroscope, accelerometer, electronic compass, etc.) and cameras, leading to new imagined and explored integration techniques. Many institutions and teachers have seen in these new tools an educational potential and have begun to develop educational strategies centered on them. Often in the past, software developments have not followed technical evolution and were usually based on exercises and basic subjects. We rarely find a program relating to work on 3D geometry, despite it being one of the most difficult concepts in mathematics for students to understand. One of the main reasons for this is no doubt the difficulty of interacting in a 3D space, usually based on a 2D device.

## C.1. Contributions

In this book, we carried out a state of the art in learning didactics and 3D geometry, and we set out the main principles of spatial structuring in children. We were thus able to describe the educational problems raised by the use of dynamic 3D geometry programs for use on desktops and of which the ergonomics were often disturbing for students. We saw that they did not create continuous links between real objects and their planar representations. Following this, we carried out a state of the art on interactions that were allowed by the use of the latest generation of MDs. We highlighted the educational benefits of each of our choices in terms of both materials and interactions. We also noted that the majority of studies linked to interactions were carried out with adults, despite Hinrichs and Carpendale [HIN 11] noting differences in interactions between adults and children.

Using a human-centered design, we studied the needs and habits of both teachers and students. First, we analyzed the pre-existing 3D geometry. Teachers generally highlighted the lack of ergonomics in classical software and, as such, students found them difficult to use correctly. In order to allow children to concentrate on what they are learning rather than on the tools they are employing, we removed as much of the technological attraction as possible, favoring content and actions. We also suggested a grammar of interactions for students aged between 9 and 15 years. We removed the use of menus and explored other possibilities of interactions. We took advantage of most of the technologies found in digital tablets in order to render the interactions more efficient and as intuitive as possible. These choices lead us to the introduction of solids into scenes using a single interaction, thanks to the use of tangible artifacts. Our evaluations of acceptability, ease of use and learning showed that:

– students accept our interactions in a very positive way;

– the children transitioned from a WIMP paradigm toward a new multi-touch one;

– our interactions turned out to be very simple and readily used by students;

– our interactions turned out to be suitable for problem solving of exercises that are in accordance with primary and middle school curriculums.

Finally, we carried out an *in situ* evaluation of the educational benefits of the introduction of our gestural grammar. For this, we developed a prototype named FINGERS (Find INteractions for GEometry learneRS), which we deployed in classrooms. These evaluations showed a significant increase in terms of students' understanding of perspectives and investigation of the concept of a solid's net. The groups that used FINGERS statistically increased their results twice as often as groups that used more classical tools such as paper–pencil or teaching solids such as polydrons. In parallel to this, we evaluated and compared adult users' cognitive load during their use of FINGERS, paper–pencil and solids during 3D geometry problem-solving exercises. It appeared that using FINGERS in problem solving of complex exercises significantly reduces the cognitive load when compared with the use of other tools. This latter study leads to new explanatory perspectives related to the educational benefits of our system.

## C.2. Perspectives

### C.2.1. *Measurement and study of cognitive load*

Leading from the experiments carried out during this study, it seemed essential to duplicate the cognitive load evaluation in students aged between 9 and 15 years. First, this experiment was the only one to have been carried out on adults (for reasons of material availability), and second because it would allow us to not only verify the results already obtained with adults but also compare the cognitive load of adults and children in solving 3D geometry problems.

### C.2.2. *Tangible vs augmented reality*

In the current teaching context, two new technologies seem promising and are increasingly the subject of studies: MDs and augmented reality. Although the latter technology only recently appeared to the general public, the term "augmented reality" is attributed to Tom Caudell, a researcher from Boeing who first used it in 1990. Augmented reality is different from virtual reality as is shown in Milgram's diagram [MIL 94], which illustrates the reality/virtuality continuum (see Figure C.1). Augmented reality consists of adding virtual elements to the real world. According to Azuma [AZU 97], augmented reality has the three following criteria:

1) integration of virtual objects into a real scene;

2) integration in real time;

3) 3D integration.

**Figure C.1.** *Milgram's reality/virtuality continuum [MIL 94]*

First, augmented reality was used to carry out maintenance tasks or difficult repairs as well as in dangerous situations such as tank maintenance [HEN 09]. Following from this, studies related to its use in education were carried out, a proportion of which related to the learning of astronomy [SHE 02, KER 06, FLE 13]. Sheldon and Hedley's studies or those of Fleck and Simon showed significant benefits to the learning of astronomy through the use of an augmented reality system whether in primary school or university.

It was important to us to explore the use of this technology in the context of 3D geometry learning. It would allow students to work on their transition from planar to 3D geometry, contrary to the approach we could have taken to our study. This complimentary approach may further increase the understanding and acquisition of spatial competencies. Finally, it would be interesting to study whether one or the other of these approaches is more relevant depending on the age of the student.

### C.2.3. *Collaborative work*

An important dimension in learning is collaborative work and help in pairs. It also seemed interesting to explore this aspect through the use of FINGERS. Karsenti and Fievez's report [KAR 13] develops this idea regarding the use of touchscreen tablets: "communication and collaboration would increase, both between the students themselves and between the students and their teacher (see [GEI 11, HEN 12, HUT 12])". We therefore wished to study more exactly the benefits to collaborative working with a menuless interface, made up of interactions following on from what we have already carried out. We wish to verify the following hypothesis: the use of an interface based on adapted interactions which would facilitate the spontaneous development of collaborative work. Furthermore, we wish to measure the educational benefits of the development of such a system, by evaluating any potential benefits to learning.

### C.2.4. *The other interactions*

Many interactions developed from our grammar are still under development and/or evaluation. We still need to finish our study by exploring, for example, color change, scaling, parametric selection of objects [VIV 14] or even planar/object intersections. Certain functionalities are integrated into FINGERS and require validation through experiments; others are currently being implemented and, thankfully, we have some more under development, which should make FINGERS more able to respond to users' needs. We must also continue to explore improvement opportunities such as spirals, which allowed us to carry out translations along three DOFs.

# Bibliography

[AGU 03] DE AGUILERA M., MENDIZ A., "Video games and education: (education in the face of a "parallel school")", *Computers in Entertainment*, vol. 1, no. 1, pp. 1–14, 2003.

[AND 92] ANDERSON R.E., "Social impacts of computing: codes of professional ethics", *Social Science Computer Review*, vol. 10, no. 4, pp. 453–469, 1992.

[ARC 13] ARCEP, La diffusion des technologies de l'information et de la communication dans la société française, CREDOC, CGE, ARCEP, press conference, December 2013.

[ARS 89] ARSAC G., "La construction du concept de figure chez les élèves de 12 ans", *Proceedings of 13th Conference of the International Group for the Psychology of Mathematics Education*, Paris: Ed. GR Didactique, vol. I, pp. 85–92, 1989.

[AUD 85] AUDIBERT G., *Représentation de l'espace et empirisme dans le problème FIL*, Publication IREM-USTL, Montpellier, 1985.

[AUD 86] AUDIBERT G., BONAFÉ F., "Apprentissage de la perspective cavalière", in RABARDEL P., WEILL-FASSINA A. (ed.), *Le dessin technique: Apprentissage, utilisations, évolutions*, Hermes, Paris, 1986.

[AUD 87] AUDIBERT G., KEITA B., "La perspective cavalière et la représentation de l'espace", in VERGNAUD G., BROUSSEAU G., HULIN M. (eds), *Didactique et acquisition des connaissances scientifiques*, La Pensée Sauvage Editions, Grenoble, 1987.

[AZU 97] AZUMA R. T., "A survey of augmented reality", *Presence: Teleoperators and Virtual Environments*, vol. 6, no. 4, pp. 355–385, August 1997.

[BAD 86] BADDELEY A.D., *Working Memory*, Clarendon Press, Oxford, 1986.

[BAG 09] BAGLIONI M., LECOLINET E., GUIARD Y., "Espace de caractérisation des interactions gestuelles physiques sur dispositifs mobiles", *Proceeding of IHM'09*, pp. 203–212, October 2009.

[BAK 03] BAKÓ M., "Different projecting methods in teaching spatial geometry", *Proceedings of the Third Conference of the European Society for Research in Mathematics Education*, 2003.

[BAL 94] BALACHEFF N., SUTHERLAND R., "Epistemological domain of validity of microworlds: the case of logo and Cabri-géomètre", in LEWIS R., MENDELSOHN P. (eds), *Lessons from Learning*, North Holland and Elsevier Science B.V., Amsterdam, 1994.

[BAL 99] BALACHEFF N., "Apprendre la preuve", in SALLANTIN J., SZCZECINIARZ J.-J. (ed.), *Le concept de preuve à la lumière de l'intelligence artificielle*, Presses Universitaires de France, Paris, 1999.

[BAR 00] BARTLETT J.F., "Rock 'n' ccroll is here to stay", *IEEE Computer Graphics and Applications*, vol. 20, no. 3, pp. 40–45, 2000.

[BAU 87] BAUTIER T., BOUDAREL J., COLMEZ F., *et al.* "Représentation plane des figures de l'espace" in VERGNAUD G., BROUSSEAU G., HULIN M. (eds), *Didactique et acquisition des connaissances scientifiques*, La Pensée Sauvage Editions, Grenoble, 1987.

[BEL 89] BELLEMAIN F., "Le logiciel Cabri-Géomètre, un nouvel environnement pour l'enseignement de la géométrie", *Cahiers du Séminaire de didactique des mathématiques de Rennes*, IREM de Rennes, 1989.

[BER 04] BERKA C., LEVENDOWSKI D.J., OLMSTEAD R.E. *et al.*, "Real-time analysis of EEG indices of alertness, cognition, and memory with a wireless EEG headset", *International Journal of Human-Computer Interaction*, vol. 17, no. 2, pp. 151–170, 2004.

[BER 07] BERKA C., LEVENDOWSKI D.J. *et al.*, "EEG correlates of task engagement and mental workload in vigilance, learning and memory tasks", *Aviation Space and Environmental Medicine*, vol. 78, no. 5, pp. B231–B244, 2007.

[BER 13a] BERTOLO D., VIVIAN R., DINET J., "A set of interactions to rotate solids in 3D geometry context", *CHI EA'13: Proceedings of CHI '13 Extended Abstracts on Human Factors in Computing Systems*, pp. 625–630, 2013.

[BER 13b] BERTOLO D., VIVIAN R., DINET J., "A set of interactions to help to resolve 3D geometry problems", *SAI'13 Proceedings of the Science and Information Conference*, pp. 738–743, 2013.

[BER 13c] BERTOLO D., VIVIAN R., DINET J., "Propositions and evaluation for a categorization of interactions in 3D geometry learning context", *International Journal of Advanced Computer Science*, vol. 3, no. 12, pp. 622–630, 2013.

[BER 14] BERTOLO D., DINET J., VIVIAN R., "Reducing cognitive workload during 3D geometry problem solving with an app on iPad", *SAI'14 Proceedings of the Science and Information Conference*, pp. 896–900, 2014.

[BIE 86] BIER E.A., "Skitters and jacks: interactive 3D positioning tools", *Workshop on Interactive 3D Graphics ACM*, pp. 183–196, 1986.

[BIE 90] BIER E.A., "Snap-dragging in three dimensions", *Symposium on Interactive 3D Graphics ACM*, pp. 193–204, 1990.

[BKO 83] BKOUCHE R., SOUFFLET M., "Axiomatique, formalisme, théorie", *Bulletin Inter-Irem Enseignement de la géométrie*, no. 23, pp. 3–24, 1983.

[BON 98] BONAFÉ F., SAUTER M., "Enseigner la géométrie dans l'espace", *Repères IREM*, no. 33, pp. 5–18, 1988.

[BOW 01] BOWMAN D.A., KRUIJFF E., LAVIOLA J. *et al*, "An introduction to 3D user interface design", *Presence*, vol. 10, no. 1, pp. 96–108, 2001.

[BRE 02] BREWSTER S., "Overcoming the lack of screen space on mobile computers", *Personal Ubiquitous Computing*, vol. 6, no. 3, pp. 188–205, 2002.

[BUX 86] BUXTON W., MYERS B., "A study in two-handed input", *ACM SIGCHI Bulletin*, vol. 17, no. 4, pp. 321–326, 1986.

[BUX 14] BUXTON W., Multi-touch systems that I have known and loved, available at http://www.billbuxton.com/multitouchOverview.html, 2014.

[CAB XX] Cabri 3D©, http://www.cabri.com/cabri-3d.html.

[CAL XX] Calque 3D©, http://www.calques3d.org/.

[CAO 09] CAO A., CHINTAMANI K.K, PANDYA A.K. *et al.*, "NASA-TLX: Software for assessing subjective mental workload", *Behavior Research Methods*, vol. 41, no. 1, pp. 113–117, 2009.

[CAR 91] CARD S.K., MACKINLAY J.D., ROBERTSON G.G., "A morphological analysis of the design space of input devices", *ACM Transactions on Information Systems*, vol. 9, no. 2, pp. 99–122, 1991.

[CHA 97] CHAACHOUA H., Fonctions du dessin dans l'enseignement de la géométrie dans l'espace. Etude d'un cas : la vie des problèmes de construction et rapports des enseignants à ces problems, PhD thesis, University Joseph Fourier, Grenoble, 1997.

[CHA 07] CHANQUOY L., TRICOT A., SWELLER J., *La charge cognitive*, A. Colin, Paris, 2007.

[CHI 06] CHITTARO L. "Visualizing information on mobile devices", *Computer*, vol. 39, no. 3, pp. 40–45, 2006.

[COH 11] COHÉ A., DÈCLE F., HACHET M., "tBox: a 3D transformation widget designed for touch-screens", *Proceedings of the SIGCHI Conference on Human Factors in Computing Systems*, pp. 3005–3008, 2011.

[COH 12] COHÉ A., HACHET M., "Understanding user gestures for manipulating 3D objects from touchscreen inputs", *Proceedings of Graphics*, pp. 157–164, 2012.

[COL 93] COLMEZ F., PARZYSZ B., "Le vu et le su dans l'évolution des dessins de pyramides du CE2 à la 2$^{nd}$", in BESSTO A., VERILLON P., BALACHEFF N. (eds), *Espaces graphiques et graphismes d'espaces*, La Pensée Sauvage Editions, Grenoble, 1993.

[DEC 09] DECLE, F., Approches Directes et Planifiées de l'Interaction 3D sur Terminaux Mobiles, PhD thesis, University of Bordeaux 1, Bordeaux, 2009.

[DEL 13] DELOITTE, Etude sur les usages mobiles: Focus sur le marché français des télécommunications, September 2013.

[DIE 01] DIETZ P., LEIGH D., "Diamondtouch: a multi-user touch technology", *Proceedings of the 14th Annual ACM Symposium on User Interface Software and Technology*, pp. 219–226, 2001.

[DOL 80] DOLLE J.M., "Recherches sur la genèse de la représentation perspective chez l'enfant", *Psychologie Française*, tome 25 no.1, pp. 3–14, 1980.

[DOL 86] DOLLE J.M., "Réflexions épistémologiques concernant la représentation graphique de l'espace tridimensionnel", in RABARDEL P., WEILL-FASSINA A. (eds), *Le dessin technique: Apprentissage, utilisations, évolutions*, Hermes, Paris, 1986.

[DON 07] DONDLINGER M.J., "Educational video game design: a review of the literature", *Journal of Applied Educational Technology*, vol. 4, no. 1, pp. 21–31, 2007.

[DUV 05] DUVAL R., "Les conditions cognitives de l'apprentissage de la géométrie : développement de la visualisation, différenciation des raisonnements et coordination de leurs fonctionnements", *Annales de Didactique et de Sciences Cognitives*, vol. 10, pp. 5–53, 2005.

[EDU 14] Éduscol, site du Ministère de l'Éducation Nationale, available at http://eduscol.education.fr/numerique/dossier/apprendre/tablette-tactile/politique-enseignement-scolaire/experimentations/les-collectivites-territoriales, 2014.

[ETH 13] ETHERINGTON D., Apple has sold over 8M iPads direct to education worldwide, with more than 1B iTunes U downloads, http:// techcrunch.com/2013/02/28/apple-has-sold-over-8m-ipads-direct-to-education-worldwide-with-more-than-1b-itunes-u-downloads/, 2013.

[FAL 13] FALLOON G., "Young students using iPads: app design and content influences on their learning pathways", *Computers & Education*, vol. 68, pp. 505–521, 2013.

[FAN 12] FAN M., PATTERSON D., SHI Y., "When camera meets accelerometer: a novel way for 3D interaction of mobile phone", *Proceedings of the 14th International Conference on Human-Computer Interaction with Mobile Devices and Services Companion*, pp. 131–136, 2012.

[FLE 13] FLECK S., SIMON G., "An augmented reality environment for astronomy learning in elementary grades: an exploratory study", *IHM'13 Proceedings of the 25th Conference on l'Interaction Homme-Machine*, pp. 9–14, 2013.

[FRA 11] FRANCONE J., NIGAY L., "Using the User's Point of View for Interaction on Mobile Devices", *Actes de la 23ème Conférence francophone sur l'Interaction Homme-Machine*, 2011.

[FRE 05] FREDERICKS T.K., CHOI S.D, HART J. *et al.*, "An investigation of myocardial aerobic capacity as a measure of both physical and cognitive workloads", *International Journal of Industrial Ergonomics*, vol. 35, no. 12, pp.1097–1107, 2005.

[GEO XX] GEOSPACE©: AID-CREEM, http://www.aid-creem.org/telechargement.htm.

[GUI 86] GUILLERMAIN H., "Approche cognitive de la genèse de la représentation graphique en perspective", in RABARDEL P., WEILL-FASSINA A. (ed.), *Le dessin technique: Apprentissage, utilisations, évolutions*, Hermes, Paris, 1986.

[GRE 08] GRENIER D., TANGUAY D., "L'angle dièdre, notion incontournable dans les constructions pratiques et théoriques des polyèdres réguliers", *Petit x*, no. 78, pp. 26–52, 2008.

[HAC 05a] HACHET M., POUDEROUX J., GUITTON P., "A camera-based interface for interaction with mobile handheld computers", *Proceedings of I3D'05 - ACM SIGGRAPH 2005 Symposium on Interactive 3D Graphics and Games*, pp. 65–71, 2005.

[HAC 05b] HACHET M., POUDEROUX J., GUITTON P., *et al.* "Tangimap - a tangible interface for visualization of large documents on handheld computers", *Proceedings of Graphics Interface*, pp. 9–15, 2005.

[HAN 05] HAN J.Y., "Low-cost multi-touch sensing through frustrated total internal reflection", *Proceedings of the 18th Annual ACM Symposium on User Interface Software and Technology, UIST '05*, pp. 115–118, 2005.

[HAN 06] HANCOCK M.S., CARPENDALE S., VERNIER F.D. *et al.*, "Rotation and translation mechanisms for tabletop interaction", *Proceedings of the First IEEE International Workshop on Horizontal Interactive Human-Computer Systems*, pp. 79–88, 2006.

[HAN 07] HANCOCK M.S., CARPENDALE S., COCKBURN A., "Shallow depth 3D interaction: design and evaluation of one-, two-, and three-touch techniques", *Proceedings of ACM CHI'2007 Conference on Human Factors in Computing Systems*, pp. 1147–1156, 2007.

[HAN 09] HANCOCK M.S., TEN CATE T., CARPENDALE S., "Sticky tools: full 6DOF force-based interaction for multi-touch tables", *Proceedings of the ACM International Conference on Interactive Tabletops and Surfaces*, pp. 133–140, 2009.

[HAN 88] HANCOCK P.A., MESHKATI N., *Human Mental Workload*, 3rd ed, Elsevier, London, 1988.

[HEN 09] HENDERSON J., FEINER S., "Evaluating the benefits of augmented reality for task localization in maintenance of an armored personnel carrier turret", *Proceedings of the International Symposium on Mixed and Augmented Reality*, pp. 135–144, 2009.

[HEN 05] HENRYSSON A., OLLILA M., BILLINGHURST M., "Mobile phone based AR scene assembly", *Proceedings of the 4th International Conference on Mobile and Ubiquitous Multimedia*, pp. 95–102, 2005.

[HEN 07] HENRYSSON A., MARSHALL J., BILLINGHURST M., "Experiments in 3D interaction for mobile phone AR", *Proceedings of the 5th International Conference on Computer Graphics and Interactive Techniques in Australia and Southeast Asia*, pp. 187–194, 2007.

[HIN 00] HINCKLEY K., PIERCE J., SINCLAIR M. *et al.*, "Sensing techniques for mobile interaction", *Proceedings of UIST'00*, pp. 91–100, 2000.

[HIN 11] HINRICHS U., CARPENDALE S., "Gestures in the wild: studying multi-touch gesture sequences on interactive tabletop exhibits", *Proceedings of the SIGCHI Conference on Human Factors in Computing Systems*, pp. 3023–3032, 2011.

[HOU 06] HOUDEMENT C., KUZNIAK A., "Paradigmes géométriques et enseignement de la géométrie", *Annales de Didactique et de Sciences Cognitives*, vol. 11, pp. 175–193, 2006.

[HOL 10] HOLZ C., BAUDISCH P., "The generalized perceived input point model and how to double touch accuracy by extracting fingerprints", *Proceedings of the 28th International Conference on Human Factors in Computing Systems*, pp. 581–590, 2010.

[HOL 11] HOLZ C., BAUDISCH P., "Understanding touch", *Proceedings of the Annual Conference on Human Factors in Computing Systems*, pp. 2501–2510, 2011.

[HUR 11] HÜRST W., HELDER M., "Mobile 3D graphics and virtual reality interaction", *Proceedings of the 8th International Conference on Advances in Computer Entertainment Technology*, 2011.

[IFE 13] IFENTHALER D., SCHWEINBENZ V., "The acceptance of tablet-PCs in classroom instruction: the teachers' perspectives", *Computers in Human Behavior*, vol. 29, pp. 525–534, 2013.

[IHA 13] IHAKA J., "Schools put tablets on stationery list", *The New Zealand Herald*, Section A4, 30 January 2013.

[JOH 11] JOHNSON J.R.R.R. *et al.*, "Drowsiness/alertness algorithm development and validation using synchronized EEG and cognitive performance to individualize a generalized model", *Biological Psychology*, vol. 87, no. 2, pp. 241–250, 2011.

[JON 10] DE JONG T., "Cognitive load theory, educational research and instructional design: some food for thought", *Instructional Science*, vol. 38, pp.105–134, 2010.

[KAM 10] KAMMER D., WOJDZIAK J., KECK M. *et al.*, "Towards a formalization of multi-touch gestures", *ACM International Conference on Interactive Tabletops and Surfaces*, pp. 49–58, 2010.

[KAR 05] KARAM M., SCHRAEFEL M.C., A taxonomy of gesture in human computer interactions. Technical Report ECSTR-IAM05-009, Electronics and Computer Science, University of Southampton, 2005.

[KAR 07] KARLSON A.K., BEDERSON B.B., CONTRERAS-VIDAL J.L., "Understanding one handed use of mobile devices" *Handbook of Research on User Interface Design and Evaluation for Mobile Technology, Idea Group Reference*, pp. 86–101, 2007.

[KAR 08] KARLSON A.K., BEDERSON B.B., "One-handed touchscreen input for legacy applications", *Proceedings of CHI'08*, pp. 1399–1408, 2008.

[KAR 13] KARSENTI T., FIEVEZ A., L'iPad à l'école: usages, avantages et défis : résultats d'une enquête auprès de 6057 élèves et 302 enseignants du Québec (Canada), Montréal, QC : CRIFPE, 2013.

[KEI 86] KEITA B., "Evaluation du rôle de l'outil graphique dans les livres des cours de physique au niveau du premier cycle universitaire", *Editions Culture Education Communication Scientifique et Evaluation*, p. 151, 1986.

[KER 06] KERAWALLA L., LUCKIN R., SELJEFLOT S. *et al.*, "Making it real: exploring the potential of augmented reality for teaching primary school science", *Virtual Reality*, vol. 10, no. 3–4, pp. 163–174, 2006.

[KER 07] KERAWALLA L., O'CONNOR J., UNDERSOOD J. *et al.*, "Exploring the potential of the Homework System and Tablet PCs to support continuity of numeracy practices between home and primary school", *Educational Media International*, vol. 44, pp. 289–303, 2007.

[KET 10] KETABDAR H., ROSHANDEL M., YÜKSEL K.A., "Towards using embedded magnetic field sensor for around mobile device 3D interaction", *Proceedings of the 12th International Conference on Human Computer Interaction with Mobile Devices and Services*, pp. 153–156, 2010.

[KIN 09] KIN K., AGRAWALA M., DEROSE T., "Determining the benefits of direct-touch, bimanual, and multifinger input on a multitouch workstation", *Proceedings of Graphics Interface 2009*, pp. 119–124, 2009.

[KIN 11] KIN K., MILLER T., BOLLENSDORFF B. *et al.*, "Eden: a professional multitouch tool for constructing virtual organic environments", *Proceedings of the 2011 Annual Conference on Human Factors in Computing Systems*, pp. 1343–1352, 2011.

[KRA 12] KRATZ S., ROHS M., GUSE D. *et al.*, "PalmSpace: continuous around-device gestures vs. multitouch for 3D rotation tasks on mobile devices", *Proceedings of the International Working Conference on Advanced Visual Interfaces*, pp. 181–188, 2012.

[KRU 05] KRUGER R., CARPENDALE S., SCOTT S D. *et al.*, "Fluid integration of rotation and translation", *Proceedings of CHI*, pp. 601–610, 2005.

[KUC 14] KUCIRKOVA N., MESSER D., SHEEHY K. *et al.*, "Children's engagement with educational iPad apps: insights from a Spanish classroom", *Computers & Education*, vol. 71, pp. 175–184, 2014.

[KUZ 06] KUZNIAK A., "Paradigmes et espaces de travail géométriques. Éléments d'un cadre théorique pour l'enseignement et la formation des enseignants en géométrie", *Canadian Journal of Science, Mathematics and Technology Education*, vol. 6.2, pp. 167–187, 2006.

[LAB 94] LABORDE C., CAPPONI B., "Cabri-géomètre constituant d'un milieu pour l'apprentissage de la notion de figure géométrique", *Recherches en Didactique des Mathématiques*, vol. 14, no. 1, pp. 165–210, 1994.

[LAB 99] LABORDE C., "L'activité instrumentée par des logiciels de géométrie dynamique", *Actes de l'école d'été de didactique des mathématiques*, pp. 203–213, 1999.

[LIS 99] LISMONT L., ROUCHE N., Formes et mouvements. Perspectives pour l'enseignement de la géométrie, technical report, Centre de Recherche pour l'Enseignement de la Géométrie, Nivelles, Belgium, 1999.

[LIA 12] LIANG H.-N., WILLIAMS C., SEMEGEN M. *et al.*, "User-defined surface+motion gestures for 3d manipulation of objects at a distance through a mobile device", *Proceedings of the 10th Asia Pacific Conference on Computer Human Interaction*, pp. 299–308, 2012.

[LIU 12] LIU J., KIN-CHUNG AU O., FU H. *et al.*, "Two-finger gestures for 6DOF manipulation of 3D objects", *Computer Graphics Forum*, vol. 31, pp. 2047–2055, 2012.

[LUQ 27] LUQUET G.-H., *Le dessin enfantin*, F. Alcan, Paris, 1927.

[MAR 13] MARTIN J., ERTZBERGER, J., "Here and now mobile learning: an experimental study on the use of mobile technology", *Computers & Education*, vol. 68, pp. 76–85, 2013.

[MAR 10a] MARTINET A., CASIEZ G., GRISONI L., "The effect of DOF separation in 3D manipulation tasks with multi-touch displays", *Proceedings of the 17th ACM Symposium on Virtual Reality Software and Technology*, pp. 111–118, 2010.

[MAR 10b] MARTINET A., CASIEZ G., GRISONI L., "The design and evaluation of 3D positioning techniques for multi-touch displays", *Proceedings of 3DUI'10, the 5th Symposium on 3D User Interfaces*, pp. 115–118, 2010.

[MAR 11] MARTINET, A., Étude de l'influence de la séparation des degrés de liberté pour la manipulation 3-D à l'aide de surfaces tactiles multipoints, PhD thesis, Université des Sciences et Technologies, Lille, 2011.

[MAS 10] MASCHIETTO M., TROUCHE L., "Mathematics learning and tools from theoretical, historical and practical points of view: the productive notion of mathematics laboratories". *ZDM – The International Journal on Mathematics Education*, vol. 42, pp. 33–47, 2010.

[MEH 82] MEHTA N., A flexible machine interface, Master's thesis, Department of Electrical Engineering, University of Toronto, 1982.

[MES 01] MESURES, Les écrans tactiles s'adaptent au besoin... grâce à la technologie. Mesures, no. 740, pp. 54– 57, 2001.

[MIC 11] MICHEL C., SANDOZ-GUERMOND F., SERNA A., "Revue de littérature sur l'évaluation de l'usage de dispositifs mobiles et tactiles ludo-éducatifs pour les jeunes enfants", *Conférence EIAH*, Mons, Belgium, 2011.

[MIL 94] MILGRAM P., "Augmented reality: A class of displays on the reality-virtuality continuum", *SPIE Volume 2351: Telemanipulator and Telepresence Technologies*, 1994.

[MIT 10] MITHALAL J., Déconstruction instrumentale et déconstruction dimensionnelle dans le contexte de la géométrie dynamique tridimensionnelle, PhD thesis, University Joseph Fourier, Grenoble, 2010.

[NAC 09] NACENTA M.A., BAUDISCH P., BENKO H. *et al.*, "Separability of spatial manipulations in multi-touch interfaces", *Proceedings of Graphics Interface*, pp. 175–182, 2009.

[NIE 86] NIELSON G.M., OLSEN D., "Direct manipulation techniques for 3D objects using 2d locator devices", *SI3D'86: Proceedings of the workshop on Interactive 3D graphics*, pp. 175–182, 1986.

[NOR 86] NORMAN D.A., DRAPER S.W., *User Centered System Design; New Perspectives on Human-Computer Interaction*, L. Erlbaum Assoc. Inc., Hillsdale, 1986.

[ISO 10] STANDARD, ISO 9241–210: 2010.

[ORF 13] ORFORD D., KEFALIDOU G., "Electronic lecturing and teaching aid using collaborative smart phones", *Science and Information Conference (SAI)*, pp. 744–750, October 2013.

[OST 87] OSTA I., "Analyse d'une séquence didactique. Représentations graphiques à l'aide d'un ordinateur comme médiateur dans l'apprentissage de notions de géométrie de l'espace", in VERGNAUD G., BROUSSEAU G., HULIN M. (eds), *Didactique et acquisition des connaissances scientifiques*, La Pensée Sauvage Editions, Grenoble, 1987.

[OVI 06] OVIATT S., "Human-centered design meets cognitive load theory: designing interfaces that help people think", *Proceedings of the 14th ACM International Conference on Multimedia (MM'06)*, pp. 871–880, October 2006.

[PAA 92] PAAS F., "Training strategies for attaining transfer of problem-solving skill in statistics: a cognitive load approach", *Journal of Educational Psychology*, vol. 84, p. 429–434, 1992.

[PAA 03] PAAS F., RENKL A., SWELLER J., "Cognitive load theory and instructional design: recent developments", *Educational Psychologist*, vol. 38, pp.1–4, 2003.

[PAR 88] PARZYSZ B., ""Knowing" vs "seeing", problems of the plane representation of space geometry figures", *Educational Studies in Mathematics*, vol. 19, pp. 79–92, 1988.

[PAR 89] PARZYSZ B., Représentations planes et enseignement de la géométrie de l'espace au lycée. Contribution à l'étude de la relation voir/savoir, PhD thesis University of Paris-7, Paris, 1989.

[PAR 91] PARZYSZ B., "Espace, géométrie et dessin. Une ingénierie didactique pour l'apprentissage, l'enseignement et l'utilisation de la perspective parallèle au lycée", *Recherches en Didactique des Mathématiques*, vol. 11, no. 2.3, pp. 211–240, 1991.

[PAR 06] PARZYSZ B., "La géométrie dans l'enseignement secondaire et en formation de professeurs des écoles : de quoi s'agit-il ? " *Quaderni di Ricerca in Didattica*, vol. 17, pp. 121–144, 2006.

[PAS 45] PASCAL B., Lettre dédicatoire à monseigneur le chancelier sur le sujet de la machine nouvellement inventée par le sieur B. P. pour faire toutes sortes d'opérations d'arithmétique par un mouvement réglé sans plume ni jetons, http://abu.cnam.fr/cgi-bin/go?machine3,1,20, 1645

[PER 10] PERRIN-GLORIAN M.-J., "L'ingénierie didactique à l'interface de la recherche avec l'enseignement", *Actes de la XVe école d'été de didactique des mathématiques*, La Pensée Sauvage, Grenoble, 2010.

[PIA 47] PIAGET J., *La psychologie de l'intelligence*, A. Colin, Paris, 1947.

[PIA 48] PIAGET J., INHELDER B., *The Child's Conception of Space*, W. W. Norton., New York, 1948.

[RAH 09] RAHMAN M., GUSTAFSON S., IRANI P. *et al.*, "Tilt techniques: investigating the dexterity of wrist-based input", *Proceedings of CHI'09*, pp.1943–1952, April 2009.

[REI 09] REISMAN J.L., DAVIDSON P.L., HAN J.Y., "A screen-space formulation for 2D and 3D direct manipulation", *Proceedings of the 22nd Annual ACM Symposium on User Interface Software and Technology*, pp. 69–78, 2009.

[RES 08] RESTREPO A., Genèse instrumentale du déplacement en géométrie dynamique chez des élèves de 6ème, PhD thesis University Joseph Fourier, Grenoble, 2008.

[RIV 08] DE LA RIVIÈRE J.-B., KERVÉGANT C., ORVAIN E. *et al.*, "Cubtile: a multi-touch cubic interface", *Proceedings of the 2008 ACM Symposium on Virtual Reality Software and Technology*, pp. 69–72, 2008.

[ROU 07] ROUDAUT A., LECOLINET E., "Un espace de classification pour l'interaction sur dispositifs mobiles", *Proceedings of the 19th International Conference of the Association Francophone d'Interaction Homme-Machine*, pp. 99–106, 2007.

[ROU 08] ROUDAUT A., HUOT S., LECOLINET E., "Taptap and magstick: improving one-handed target acquisition on small touch-screens", *Proceedings of the Working Conference on Advanced Visual Interfaces*, pp. 146–153, 2008.

[ROU 09] ROUDAUT A., BAGLIONI M., LECOLINET E., "TimeTilt: using sensor-based gestures to travel through multiple applications on a mobile device", *Proceedings of Interact'08*, pp. 830–834, August 2009.

[SAU 11] SAURET Q., FRANCONE J., NIGAY L., "Interaction sur Dispositifs Mobiles : glisser-déposer devant/derrière bi-manuel", *Actes Complémentaires de la 23e Conférence Francophone sur l'Interaction Homme-Machine (IHM)*, 2011.

[SCH 08] SCHMIDT R., SINGH K., BALAKRISHNAN R., "Sketching and composing widgets for 3D manipulation", *Computer Graphics Forum*, vol. 27, no. 2, pp. 301–310, 2008.

[SCO 11] SCODITTI A., VINCENT T., COUTAZ J., *et al.* "TouchOver: decoupling positioning from selection on touch-based handheld devices", *23rd French Speaking Conference on Human-Computer Interaction*, 2011.

[SHE 02] SHELTON B.E., HEDLEY N.R. "Using augmented reality for teaching Earth-Sun relationships to undergraduate geography students", *The First IEEE International Augmented Reality Toolkit Workshop*, Damstadt, Germany, 2002.

[SHE 04] SHELTON B.E., HEDLEY N.R., "Exploring a cognitive basis for learning spatial relationships with augmented reality", *Technology, Instruction, Cognition and Learning*, vol.°1, no. 4, pp. 323–357, 2004.

[SHE 09] SHEN E.E., TSAI S.D., CHU H. *et al.*, "Double-side multi-touch input for mobile devices", *Proceedings of the 27th International Conference Extended Abstracts on Human Factors in Computing Systems*, pp. 4339–4344, 2009.

[SHI 11] SHIN D.-H., SHIN Y.-J., CHOO H. *et al.*, "Smartphones as smart pedagogical tools: Implications for smartphones as u-learning devices", *Computers in Human Behavior*, vol. 27, no. 6, pp. 2207–2214, 2011.

[SOU 12] SOURY-LAVERGNE S., MASCHIETTO M., "A la découverte de la "pascaline" pour l'apprentissage de la numération décimale", *Colloque Copirelem*, Quimper, 2012.

[SWE 88] SWELLER J., "Cognitive load during problem solving: effects of learning", *Cognitive Science*, vol. 12, pp. 257–285, 1988.

[TRO 10] TROUCHE L., DRIJVERS P., "Handheld technology for mathematics education: flashback into the future", *ZDM – The International Journal on Mathematics Education,* vol. 42, pp. 667–681, 2010.

[TSA 02] TSANG M., FITZMAURICE G.W., KURTENBACH G. *et al.,* "Boom Chameleon: Simultaneous capture of 3D viewpoint, voice and gesture annotations on a spatially-aware display", *Proceedings of the 15th Annual ACM Symposium on User Interface Software and Technology (UIST '02),* pp. 698–698, 2002.

[VAN 99] VAN LABEKE N., Prise en compte de l'usager enseignant dans la conception des EIAO. Illustration dans Calques 3D, PhD thesis University Henri Poincaré, Nancy, 1999.

[VIV 12] VIVIAN R., DINET J., BERTOLO D., "Spring: a solution for managing the third DOF with tactile interface", *Proceedings of the 10th Asia Pacific Conference on Computer Human Interaction (APCHI'12),* pp. 251–258, 2012.

[VIV 14] VIVIAN R., BERTOLO D., DINET J., "Definition of tactile interactions for a multi-criteria selection in a virtual world", *International Journal of Advanced Computer Science & Applications,* vol. 5, no. 12, pp. 65–71, 2014.

[VOG 07] VOGEL D., BAUDISCH P., "Shift: a technique for operating pen-based interfaces using touch", *Proceedings of the SIGCHI Conference on Human Factors in Computing Systems,* pp. 657–666, 2007.

[VOG 09] VOGEL D., CUDMORE M., CASIEZ G. *et al.,* "Hand occlusion with tablet-sized direct pen input", *Proceedings of the 27th International Conference on Human Factors in Computing Systems (CHI'09),* pp. 557–566, 2009.

[WAN 09] WANG F., REN X., "Empirical evaluation for finger input properties in multi-touch interaction", *Proceedings of the 27th International Conference on Human Factors in Computing Systems,* pp. 1063–1072, 2009.

[WIG 06] WIGDOR D., LEIGH D., FORLINES C. *et al.,* "Under the table interaction", *Proceedings of the 19th Annual ACM Symposium on User Interface Software and Technology,* pp. 268, 2006.

[WIG 07] WIGDOR D., FORLINES C., BAUDISCH P. *et al.,* "Lucid touch: a see-through mobile device", *Proceedings of the 20th Annual ACM Symposium on User Interface Software and Technology (UIST'07),* pp. 269–278, 2007.

[WOB 09] WOBBROCK J.O., RINGEL MORRIS M., WILSON A.D., "User-defined gestures for surface computing", *Proceedings of the SIGCHI Conference on Human Factors in Computing Systems,* pp. 1083–1092, 2009.

[WOL 81] WOLFELD J.A., Real time control of a robot tactile sensor, MSc Thesis, Moore School of Electrical Engineering, Philadelphia, PA, 1981.

# Index

Other titles from

in

Information Systems, Web and Pervasive Computing

## 2016

BEN CHOUIKHA Mona
*Organizational Design for Knowledge Management*

LAGRAÑA Fernando
*E-mail and Behavioral Changes: Uses and Misuses of Electronic Communications*

KITAJIMA Munéo
*Memory and Action Selection in Human–Machine Interaction (Human–Machine Interaction Set – Volume 1)*

VENTRE Daniel
*Information Warfare – 2^{nd} edition*

## 2015

ARDUIN Pierre-Emmanuel, GRUNDSTEIN Michel, ROSENTHAL-SABROUX Camille
*Information and Knowledge System (Advances in Information Systems Set – Volume 2)*

BÉRANGER Jérôme
*Medical Information Systems Ethics*

BRONNER Gérald
*Belief and Misbelief Asymmetry on the Internet*

IAFRATE Fernando
*From Big Data to Smart Data*
*(Advances in Information Systems Set – Volume 1)*

KRICHEN Saoussen, BEN JOUIDA Sihem
*Supply Chain Management and its Applications in Computer Science*

NEGRE Elsa
*Information and Recommender Systems*
*(Advances in Information Systems Set – Volume 4)*

POMEROL Jean-Charles, EPELBOIN Yves, THOURY Claire
*MOOCs*

SALLES Maryse
*Decision-Making and the Information System (Advances in Information Systems Set – Volume 3)*

SAMARA Tarek
*ERP and Information Systems: Integration or Disintegration*
*(Advances in Information Systems Set – Volume 5)*

## 2014

DINET Jérôme
*Information Retrieval in Digital Environments*

HÉNO Raphaële, CHANDELIER Laure
*3D Modeling of Buildings: Outstanding Sites*

KEMBELLEC Gérald, CHARTRON Ghislaine, SALEH Imad
*Recommender Systems*

MATHIAN Hélène, SANDERS Lena
*Spatio-temporal Approaches: Geographic Objects and Change Process*

PLANTIN Jean-Christophe
*Participatory Mapping*

VENTRE Daniel
*Chinese Cybersecurity and Defense*

## 2013

BERNIK Igor
*Cybercrime and Cyberwarfare*

CAPET Philippe, DELAVALLADE Thomas
*Information Evaluation*

LEBRATY Jean-Fabrice, LOBRE-LEBRATY Katia
*Crowdsourcing: One Step Beyond*

SALLABERRY Christian
*Geographical Information Retrieval in Textual Corpora*

## 2012

BUCHER Bénédicte, LE BER Florence
*Innovative Software Development in GIS*

GAUSSIER Eric, YVON François
*Textual Information Access*

STOCKINGER Peter
*Audiovisual Archives: Digital Text and Discourse Analysis*

VENTRE Daniel
*Cyber Conflict*

## 2011

BANOS Arnaud, THÉVENIN Thomas
*Geographical Information and Urban Transport Systems*

DAUPHINÉ André
*Fractal Geography*

LEMBERGER Pirmin, MOREL Mederic
*Managing Complexity of Information Systems*

PAPY Fabrice
*Information Science*

RIVARD François, ABOU HARB Georges, MERET Philippe
*The Transverse Information System*

ROCHE Stéphane, CARON Claude
*Organizational Facets of GIS*

## 2008

BRUGNOT Gérard
*Spatial Management of Risks*

FINKE Gerd
*Operations Research and Networks*

GUERMOND Yves
*Modeling Process in Geography*

KANEVSKI Michael
*Advanced Mapping of Environmental Data*

MANOUVRIER Bernard, LAURENT Ménard
*Application Integration: EAI, B2B, BPM and SOA*

PAPY Fabrice
*Digital Libraries*

## 2007

DOBESCH Hartwig, DUMOLARD Pierre, DYRAS Izabela
*Spatial Interpolation for Climate Data*

SANDERS Lena
*Models in Spatial Analysis*

## 2006

CLIQUET Gérard
*Geomarketing*

CORNIOU Jean-Pierre
*Looking Back and Going Forward in IT*

DEVILLERS Rodolphe, JEANSOULIN Robert
*Fundamentals of Spatial Data Quality*

CPSIA information can be obtained at www.ICGtesting.com
Printed in the USA
BVOW06*1946040716

454276BV00002B/2/P